Daring

to

Date Again

Hi neighbor!
You knew my story
from the beginning

Ann

Published 2014
Printed in the United States of America
ISBN: 978-1-63152-909-2
Library of Congress Control Number: 2014938016

Book design by Stacey Aaronson

For information, address:
She Writes Press
1563 Solano Ave #546
Berkeley, CA 94707

Daring
to Date
Again

a memoir

Ann Anderson Evans

SWP

SHE WRITES PRESS

To *Prince Charming*

20something swm seeks swf over 60

hey there 20something,
how do you know about
a raging libido lately
birthed after that dark
secret thing called marriage
and 7,376 nights spent waiting
for something that never arrived?
fyi this 16-year-old mind
trapped in a vintage body
turns every which way,
sends midnight messages:
60something swf no longer
knows what's for dinner or where,
precisely, she left a certain
unsung verse – hanging, perhaps,
off the budding branch of a
jacaranda tree.
btw the sky,
on certain crepuscular days,
shines all orange with promise.

~Janet Ward

The names and other identifiers of most of the people I have written about have been changed out of respect for their privacy. Everything in the book really happened.

· I ·

The Starting Point

hen a sixty-year-old, twice-divorced woman starts to date again, she's not pinning her hopes on an invitation to the prom. She is financially stable and professionally credentialed. She is a matriarch, a pillar of her church, a member of a choir. She has children and neighbors who might disapprove. She has a lot at stake.

For me, marriage had lost its sheen after two divorces. My needs had been whittled down to conversation and sex. I could get conversation from my friends or colleagues; finding sex was a riskier matter. The term "friends with benefits" sounded juvenile. "Having an affair" sounded illicit. "Getting married" sounded terrifying. "Romp in the hay" was more like it.

What I knew of love was shrouded in rules and expectations soon to crumble under the weight of new experience. Soon, the anonymous Internet would make it safe for men (and me) to reveal thoughts and wishes that had long lain unearthed. Distance would shrink to a simple click, and I would commune with hundreds of men.

I had believed my thoughts and desires were not shared by others. Then I learned that widowed Great Aunt Tony, who died around 1975, had been much more than the begirdled figure I remembered sitting up straight in her chair. "She had some kind of romance with Grant Crane. He used to live out on Longacre Road someplace. I don't know exactly what happened there." It comforted me that I was not alone as I stepped into a world where I felt I was risking everything.

· 2 ·

At the Rope's End

O n a hot September afternoon in 2003 I left the rest of the picnickers and walked to the secluded nude beach where a hundred or so naked people were casually fishing, swimming, and talking. I took off my clothes, folded them, weighted them on my towel with a stone, and eased into the cool water of a Vermont lake.

As I swam, my shoulders moved freely without restraining straps. Without a bathing suit, the temperature of my tummy was the same as my back, my legs. The water streamed against my body like a caress. I swam and swam, then lay on my towel to dry off in the enveloping sun. I had come to a weekend at the Rowe Camp and Conference Center to find someone to have sex with. I might have said "companionship," but really, it was for sex. Twelve years of celibacy had become intolerable. I was turning off the lights in my living room and dancing wildly alone. (I didn't want to be seen by the people walking their dogs outside my house. They would think I was deranged.) I avoided romantic movies because they upset me so; my sleep was disturbed by erotic dreams. My kindling body burst into flame at the slightest frisson of affection. I was even ambushed by an orgasm while lying stock still on my bed thinking about a man I had become obsessed with. I didn't know that was possible! I was afraid that my anguished body would force me to do something stupid, and I had already done enough stupid things in my life.

The delicious liberty of celibacy had been replaced by a cavewoman need for sex. But my last date had been nineteen years ago, when I met my second husband, and I had no idea where to begin. My cousin had given me memberships to the Rowe Center for two years, saying I should go there, the people were nice. Here I was.

Even after an eventful romantic life, I felt unprepared. Every bit of instruction or advice I'd ever received about sex was nonsense, but I wasn't sure what the truth was. When I was growing up, my mother told me, "Men are animals," which frightened me. On my first dates the pawing and groping seemed beneath me. Later, I knew they could do you some real damage if you got pregnant, and still later, I learned they could suck you dry. But wasn't I an animal too? The more I resisted sex, the more animal-like I became.

My father said, "Men like fast women, but they don't marry them." His paradigm for such a person was "Dirty Ankles McGee," a fun gal who hung around the military training camp in California where my father had served as a training officer during the Second World War. His words frightened me too. For a girl growing up in the 1950s, marriage was all there was. Without it, I'd be desiccated, cut off from society. The world marched in pairs, and I wouldn't have anyone to go to the movies with except another spinster, another old maid.

My second husband threw in a warning when we divorced: "There's no more chance than a snowball in hell that a woman over forty will ever marry again." Yes, men prefer younger women—everybody knows that—and I was almost fifty when we divorced. Life without another marriage was better than life with my second husband, but life isn't all-or-nothing, either-or. Given my skittish pessimism, I wasn't surprised that my celibacy had gone unchallenged by the slightest interest from a man, proving that I was over hill—but unless I wanted to dance alone in my dark living room for the rest of my life, I would have to seek out the touch of a man. I would have to *seek* it.

After my beautiful swim, I walked back to the picnic ground and screwed up the courage to tell a retired nuclear physicist, Roger, that I had never ridden on a motorcycle, and asked him to take me back to the farmhouse on his. He seemed happy to do it, and I climbed up, wrapped my arms around him, and relaxed into the tight embrace.

· 3 ·

My First Dance

Over dinner that evening, I chatted with Lenny, a curly-haired, divorced carpenter specializing in historic renovation. He had a kind, quirky manner and an interesting fashion sense—black velvet jacket, bright pink shirt.

After dinner, we folded up the tables in the dining hall and a local band played rock and roll. People who couldn't dance worth a damn were welcome on the floor, their out-of-sync bodies bobbling around as joyfully as everyone else's. In one day, I had flirted with two different men, and that made me giddy. The future was looking bright—I was wearing the Red Shoes, dancing alone, only this time in public.

On a break, I saw the shadowy outline of someone looking in from the dark deck outside the dining hall. I was struck by this person's hesitation. Moments later, my dinner partner Lenny came in wearing fishnet stockings and heels, a scarlet bow around his waist, a flouncy black skirt, and a corset top. He had a large red bow in his curly hair.

He came straight over to me and grabbed my hand, pulling me onto the dance floor. His cheeks had rounds of bright rouge that made his lipstick seem more scarlet. He had powdered over his whiskers, and his long eyelashes were coated with mascara.

I was wearing sneakers, blue jeans, and a plaid lumberjack's shirt and felt ridiculous, but he was glowing, so I said, "You look beautiful, Lenny."

"Thank you! Thank you! I *feel* beautiful. This is the first time in my life that I have ever gone out in public dressed like this, and I feel wonderful! Do you believe that? The first time."

I was humbled and flattered that I was the first woman he had danced with as his natural self. He had been coming to Rowe for years, gotten comfortable there, and had chosen this night to emerge from heaven knows what misery. I didn't have the heart to put him off, though my instincts were objecting loudly.

He pulled me close, his rouged cheek against mine. I chattered and laughed to cover my discomfort. Was he gay and just having dress-up fun, or was he a heterosexual transvestite who was making a pass at me? It seemed the latter.

Yes, here he was! A man who wanted to have sex with me! But I just couldn't soften my body against his satin self. When the dance was over, he put his forehead on mine; I squeezed his hands and said, "That was great," and went off to get a glass of water. I just couldn't do any more.

Seeing how I love silk, and how much other women love satin and jewels, it seemed churlish to deny Lenny the pleasure of wearing them too. Too bad that men in lipstick make me feel uncomfortable in a place not governed by my mind. I was disappointed that the first man who had asked me to dance in twelve years was wearing a skirt, but it felt wonderful to dance with any man again.

• • •

NO MIRACLES HAPPENED during my weekend at Rowe—or maybe they did. A little stone moved inside me and opened my way forward.

Back at work, Keith, a husky, blue-eyed, ukulele-playing paralegal, began to drift by my desk daily. He was ten years younger than me, so it never occurred to me that he might want me.

Keith was brilliant: he could remember baseball statistics, play songs *vivace* on the ukulele, recite poetry, add up numbers in his head, read text in a mirror, and quote famous philosophers. Being a secretary was boring, and he brought some levity and variety to my days. But there was a tide of anger in him, and a vulgar side, and I didn't want to be alone with him, not even for lunch.

One day he sent me an e-mail: *Pardon my venturing a terribly porcine, lascivious and salacious affirmation. I think you're hot, irrespective of your age. oink. oink.*

So he really *was* strange—the man who liked older women, the loner caught up in a sick fantasy. He was such an interesting mix of the Good and the Awful that I was tempted to take him up on his offer of a baseball game or a little ice skating in the park, but then he would poke the index finger of one hand through a circle made of the thumb and first finger of his other hand, or display his tongue, and my fragile fantasy would collapse. I would have to look further.

· 4 ·

Busting Out

My ninety-two-year-old mother had a heart attack, and then another, and the next few months were full of her brushes with death. Two years before, when she was ninety, I had found her standing on a footstool changing a lightbulb in the ceiling. Seeing her tall, spindly body profiled clearly atop the kitchen stool, swaying more than she thought it was, her hand shaking as she screwed in the lightbulb, it had been clear to me then that her decline was beginning. She'd been a reliable mother, erring toward the cool side, who had handled my divorces with understanding and written checks that lifted me out of messes. I owed her. So I sold my house and moved in.

My intention was to provide security and comfort, and a parade of candidates to be my first sex partner in twelve years would not have sat well with her. So my celibacy continued unchallenged.

One evening my best friend Greta's husband, Fred, and I watched a Sweet Sixteen basketball game in the basement, whooping and hollering. At the time, Fred was an editor at *The New York Times* and well-set financially, but he is a miserly sort. Their television was a derelict castaway that he'd salvaged from the street, so my mother's big-screen television was a treat. After Fred left, I came up to the kitchen, where my mother was looking out the window slowly eating an orange, and she said, "I admire you for being able to have a relationship with a man without, you know . . ."

Was "you know" sex?

"What do you mean?" I asked.

"Well . . ." I hung on her long pause. "I just admire you."

Having sex with my best friend's husband would have been such a betrayal that not doing it didn't seem praiseworthy. Did she think that was what other people did? She didn't want to talk about it.

SHE WAS DEFIANT as she aged—jumping over snowbanks at eighty-nine, indefatigably going to her committee meetings, exercising daily on her ski machine in the basement—but the downward spiral inched along. Three years after the lightbulb incident she was spending more time in the hospital than at home. The end was near, so we stuffed my brothers and their families into the house on Edgecliff Road and took turns on a twenty-four-hour vigil, with the teenage grandchildren taking the night shift. Then there was the final trip home into hospice care. I thought I would be undone by having to oversee my mother's death, but the hospice nurses allowed me to shuck my responsibilities and rest. She died the day after Valentine's Day, 2003. I think we sent her off calm and peaceful, even happy. Or maybe it was the morphine.

I was played out. Months of stress had eaten away about twenty pounds. One morning, I stepped out of the shower and glimpsed myself in the slightly steamed-up mirror over the sink. The morning was dark and only the muted shower light was on behind the curtain. The spider veins in my thighs disappeared in the misty reflection and my skin turned milky and smooth. I looked brown-haired, shapely, and youthful.

The light had touched me and made me bloom. In the mirror was a woman who could wear fitted blouses and slinky black dresses. She might even wear heels and tower over others, just for fun. I liked her.

At the reception after the memorial service a few weeks later, a fortyish, tall screenwriter with dark, curly hair named Michael darted over and introduced himself. He was very thin and slightly bowlegged. He had read my mother's obituary in the newspaper and saw a screenplay in her life, especially the incongruity of her as a newly widowed fifty-eight-year-old sophomore student at Columbia University when anti-war protests convulsed the university and the country in 1968. It was worth talking about, and I gave Michael my phone number.

Then it was all over. My mother was dead, over a hundred people had attended her memorial service, and my brothers were back in their own homes. I continued living in the house, hypersensitive to sounds, daunted by my new stewardship of house and garden, haunted by my mother's instructions to keep the thermostat at sixty-eight and to have dinner at seven. I didn't touch her favorite magazines or rearrange the kitchen cupboards. My mood swung between scared, sad, and relieved.

Michael phoned and was the first person outside the family to visit me after my mother's death. I rushed up the steep hill from the train with only enough time to hang up a stray coat and put the breakfast dishes in the dishwasher before he arrived at seven on the dot. He was freshly shaven and wore tailored pants, shined shoes, and a silk shirt that clung. We chatted in the living room, and then he asked if I'd like to go out for a bite to eat. I was tired, and invited him to some scrambled eggs and toast in the kitchen instead. I thought I caught a coy look in his eye, but I told myself that couldn't be true. He was somewhere around twenty years younger than I was and couldn't possibly have the least thought of seduction. Nah. The dam between my libido and younger men was still fully intact. But I did notice how attractive he was. He had energy in every feature—a sharp nose, thin mouth, dark, inquiring eyes. He was thin and springy, coiled to move quickly and with purpose.

Over supper, we talked about the proposed screenplay. His vision of my mother transformed from a conventional matron into a radical revolutionary was overblown. I said, "She was a very liberal-minded woman, but she said that the only thing she remembered about the campus protests was how annoyed she was that she couldn't get to the library." The talk of a screenplay petered out.

While I was brewing the coffee he asked, "How old are you?" It took me only a second to decide whether I would tell him the truth. It was lies and false expectations about relationships and sex that had harmed me in the past, so I said, "Sixty. Just last month."

He was tongue-tied. "Wow. I thought you were about fifty, mid-fifties at the most. Sixty? That's unbelievable." He reacted as if I had confessed that I was really a man.

He changed the subject instantly, telling me about his years in Beverly Hills writing almost-successful screenplays while smoking too much marijuana, and his hopes for a new career now that he had come back East. He hoped he didn't have to fall back on his law degree.

Around eleven, he left. I had closed the door and started turning off the lights when the doorbell rang. It was Michael, smiling broadly. "We parted too coldly. I want to hug you."

Our good-night hug on the darkened landing lasted

seconds, but seemed a very long time. For years I had been avoiding close contact with men. I could not escape feeling the muscles of his gym-trained back, hard under my hands.

"I knew you'd be a good hugger," he said, kissing my cheek. Remaining composed was like holding my finger over a flame without screaming.

Michael and I were both free of commitments, and we were both lonely. (He was living in his mother's basement.) So we began to go places together. Michael wanted children and was looking for a woman to bear them, which counted me out, so we weren't exactly "dating," but it was similar. We talked and talked—in cafés, theatres, and once in my car until the sun rose. I could stay out as late as I pleased; there was nobody waiting for me at home.

He revealed a life devoid of stable commitment to either a person or a job. After two tough divorces I had learned my lesson thoroughly: I wanted a man who was sane and solvent. Michael was on medication for anxiety, sleeplessness, and obsessive-compulsiveness. He was also on unemployment.

· 5 ·

Intro to a New World

Michael got me out of the house and made me question my assumptions. He was erratic, abrasive, and rattled on about himself for hours, but he also introduced me to Radiohead and Eva Cassidy's music; danced with me on the tiny dance floor in South Park, a loud, Montclair bar filled with twenty- and thirty-year-olds; took long walks with me along the western side of the Hudson River just above the George Washington Bridge; and did exercises with me in the Bronx Botanical Garden.

From the time I was a teenager, I had thought that "normal" men sought out younger women. In my early dating years I would never have dated a man younger than I was. It seemed basic biology—the way it had always been. Between 1970 and 1992 I was married or living with a mate and did not pay attention to other peoples' dating habits. Demi Moore and

Elizabeth Taylor married men much younger than they, but they were celebrities, measured by a different yardstick.

I could not fathom the motives of Lenny and Keith. I was inclined to dismiss them out of hand as men cursed with an awkward fetish. Michael was in-between. Since he was neither sane nor solvent, I wouldn't have considered a serious relationship with him, yet we were spending a lot of time together. Each of us wished for some other kind of long-term companion, but in the meantime, we were friends.

If I met another younger man who was sane and solvent and wanted a family, what would I do? That November, I heard about a fifty-seven-year-old woman, Aleta St. James, giving birth to twins. Borrowing eggs and sperm to create children was no longer a miracle. Surrogate mothers were carrying babies for women who couldn't carry one themselves. Charlie Chaplin and Paul McCartney had both had children at an advanced age and nobody seemed indignant or scolding. Now women could do the same. This was the first time in the history of the world that a woman of my age could entertain such thoughts. Women's equality was expanding to places I had never expected.

The answer to my question was a convoluted list of "what-ifs." The health, family situation, financial status, and attitude of some women might encourage having a baby at sixty, but my own pioneer fantasy was snuffed out by my fondness for a good night's sleep and memories of increasingly heavy children soulfully reaching to me, crying, "Uppy, uppy."

In June, my daughter was appearing in a play at a tiny Greenwich Village theater on MacDougal Street, and I asked Michael if he'd like to meet me there. At curtain time there was no sign of him, so I went into the dark theater alone, irritated, and disappointed. In the middle of the first act, he slid into the seat beside me, whispering that he'd gotten lost.

After the play, a group of us came out into a warm New

York evening, giddily après-theater. One of the cast members gamboled along with one foot on the curb, the other in the street, singing a French song and steadying himself like a tightrope walker.

We streamed to the cramped bar of the Washington Square Hotel. The tables fit four wine glasses and a basket of nuts. A bar at one end of the room was rimmed by a black leather armrest. There were four bar stools, which people had moved around to suit their conversations. Behind the bar were glass shelves with shiny glasses on them, lit aquamarine from below.

I felt hip and happy. I was down to size 8 slacks, loved my new spiky punk haircut, and, for once, I wasn't alone at a party. Michael leaned over my chair. "What do you want to drink?"

"How about a glass of red wine?"

"Be right back." He patted my shoulder.

When he came back he handed me the glass of wine and smiled at the cast members sitting opposite. A shapely brunette softly placed her hand on the banquette next to her, and Michael sat there instead of sitting next to me. I was mortified. I had been brought up to believe that you danced with the one who brought you.

I ignored him for a while, and when I looked over again, he was standing at the bar sideways, holding a drink, his foot on the bar rail, in conversation with a small, unsmiling Asian woman seated on a stool, her feet barely reaching the rungs. Everything about her was my opposite—she was tiny, Asian, reserved, and conservatively dressed. Michael seemed comfortable, but I was seething and hurt. Was this really how dating was done these days? We weren't on a typical date, but only the two of us knew that.

I went to the ladies' room to think. Maybe my standards of politeness were no more valid in 2003 than my mother's were to me. Still, I felt like a procurer for Michael, introducing him to a fishbowl full of attractive women.

Back in my seat, I tried to catch Michael's eye, but his eyes were locked onto the unsmiling woman's. I told my daughter, "I think I've had enough."

"What do you mean?"

"I'm going home."

"You're leaving?" Her eyes snapped open wide.

"That's right."

She studied at me for a few seconds, waiting for an explanation, which I didn't give. "Okay. I'll walk you to your car."

She told me later that her friends thought I "had balls" for publicly walking out on Michael, but I didn't agree. There were a dozen more graceful ways I could have handled the situation. I was rusty, clumsy. The dating world had changed during the decades I'd spent buried in marriage, child-rearing, and celibacy, and I now had a lot to learn.

Michael sent me agitated e-mails wondering what had happened to me, and we met for dinner a few nights later. When I told him how offended I had been, especially because it had happened in front of my daughter, he didn't understand my point. "I'm sorry you feel this way, but we're not in that kind of relationship. Why shouldn't I talk to any woman I want to talk to?"

"If you go someplace with a woman, you're her escort."

"You mean I'm chained to her? Come on."

"It doesn't mean you can't have a conversation with another woman, but it's different if you hit on them."

"I wasn't hitting on either one of them! Nothing happened!"

"You looked like you were hitting on them." I was tying myself up in rhetorical knots.

"That's a distinction without a difference." He was shaking his head.

He was right, sort of, but I still didn't like it. We agreed to disagree over the incident, and resumed our almost-dates, but I didn't want to be embarrassed again, and our attachment waned.

Michael was insulting sometimes, rude sometimes, but he was unwaveringly fond of me and told me so. He could have been even crazier and ruder and I would still have been fond of him. With every new Michael adventure, I could feel the mold around me breaking. I was pecking my way out of the egg.

· 6 ·

Preparing to Launch

Over wine and an excellent dinner at her house, I told my best friend Greta that I would like to date again, but didn't know where to find eligible men. I was so unsure about whether what I wanted to do was normal that I hadn't told her about Michael or the other men I had met. I spoke in vague generalities.

I was anticipating a slightly naughty reply—maybe a joke, or perhaps the story of a friend who finally found erotic bliss with her plumber—but Greta reacted thoughtfully. This wasn't a joke to me, and I was grateful to her for understanding that. "You haven't dated in a long time, have you?"

"Twelve years. A friend of mine said her grandmother told her she hadn't had sex since her husband died. It had been something like thirty years. I don't want to be like her, just giving up and growing old, keeping my body locked away. I don't want to act like I'm dead."

"Twelve years is too long. Really. I suppose Mother Theresa got affection from her patients or whatever you call them, but you're a secretary! Who are you going to get it from," she teased, "a bunch of lawyers?"

That was a joke worth laughing at. The law firm where I worked only hired the best students from the best schools, yet they were a gnarly mix of neuroses and obsessions. The only one I'd had even the smallest crush on had turned out to be gay. "That's all I need—to lose my job because I dated one of the attorneys. If anything went wrong, you know who would get fired."

"You, of course."

"Of course. And outside the law firm, there's been something wrong with all the men I've met."

"Like what?"

"One lived far away, one was a transvestite, two of them are probably crazy."

Greta doesn't laugh a whole lot, but my remark hit her smack in the funny bone; she put her head in her hand and laughed her barking laugh. "It's been a long time since I dated, but you're bringing back my past."

From her back deck she looked down at her flowers, the ones a groundhog had been eating. She reflected a few minutes, then said, "I think you should make it a research project. Date a hundred men."

"Where would I find a hundred men? I can't find even one!"

Greta gets down to the nub of things fast. "What are you looking for? Do you want someone to go to dinner and the movies with? To travel with? To marry? What do you want?"

I gave a cynical little laugh. "I don't think someone who's been married and divorced twice should be looking for marriage again."

"Give yourself a break! You've been responsible, you've

been a good mother, you've got a good job. Why not?"

"Okay. I guess it's more than that. When I was married, I was always thinking about what my husband would want for dinner or wanted to do this weekend. I censored my wishes so they would conform to his, and then, after a while, I lost touch with what I would really wish for. Now that I live alone, I can do as I please, and the last thing in the world I want is to be married again."

I lacked the courage to tell the truth, but Greta was looking at me with such attentiveness. She really wanted to know what I thought, so I dove in. "What I want right now is sex."

Greta said simply, "Well then, start there."

Driving back home, I strategized. Beginning with sex was apparently a sensible choice, not a sign of primitive helplessness. The challenge lay elsewhere. My previous choices in men had been so bad that I didn't trust my judgment, so I would have to date men I hadn't considered before. Instead of finding people I "had a lot in common with," I would have to look for my unicorn in new places. What did men want? What were they really like? How many different kinds of men would I be compatible with? Did I want marriage? An affair? One man? Two? Would I go out with married men? Were my ideas about sex too narrow, too based on my upbringing and not on the real world? Did men respect women they had sex with? What did I have that men wanted? What were my weaknesses? Did other older women date? Were they considered pitiful? Where were the men? Did older men only want younger women? It would take a while to answer all these questions.

I would begin by looking for a man my age or a little older who still had some spark. I knew some sparkly, interesting men my age—all married, but at least I knew they existed. I didn't need dozens of men, only one, but Greta was right, I might have to meet a hundred others to find him.

A Rendezvous with Technology

A friend at work met someone through an Internet dating site. She was the first person I knew who had done that. The process seemed dangerous and awkward, and although as a secretary I worked with computers, Internet dating seemed fraught with new technological challenges. Then I heard a radio advertisement for a dating site called the Classical Music Lovers' Exchange. How dangerous could Mozart lovers be?

I scrolled through the profiles on CMLE.com, engaged in some e-mail conversations, and a few days later I spoke on the phone with a retired seventy-year-old divorced man who lived on the Upper West Side of Manhattan. "Boy, I'm glad to talk to you," he said in a scratchy voice, "I was about to give up on this Internet dating thing. I haven't met anybody at all."

"I'm new to this too."

"Uh huh."

There was a pause, which I broke. "Tell me about yourself. I guess you like music or you wouldn't be on this site."

"Sure I like music. Not the kind of music I hear all the time these days. Those young people—I listen to their music and it sounds like hyenas screeching, it's just so wretched. They've never heard of Mozart, much less Wagner. I mean, have your own music, but at least you ought to know a little bit about history. Don't you agree?"

Given my newfound delight in Radiohead, we wouldn't be able to discuss even our supposed mutual interest in music.

The Internet is only going to bring me losers, I thought, *and when it comes to romance, I'm a loser myself.* Another dead end.

Then my phone beeped as another call came in, and I excused myself from the depressing conversation.

It was Stuart, a fifty-eight-year-old psychologist also from CMLE.com. He offered to drive the fifteen miles from Ridgewood to Montclair to take me to dinner, and asked me to choose a restaurant. I appreciated his gallantry. This felt like a real date, the kind my friends had in high school. It wasn't true love or lustful fantasy; it was just a date.

Stuart and I joked about our lack of skill getting photos onto our computers, so we agreed to exchange them by mail. It was warm and fun to joke about our technological backwardness, but when I hung up the phone I felt more like a loser. Internet dating was for younger people who knew computer tricks. Why was I entering a world I was completely unprepared for?

Because nothing else was working.

A few days later, Stuart's picture arrived. It showed a graying, slightly overweight man smiling over a birthday cake. He didn't look like the kind of guy who would knock me off my feet, but he didn't look like an ax murderer or an utter bore. If I didn't like him, I'd only have to make it through a single date.

· 8 ·

My First Date

On the afternoon of my date with Stuart, I tried on all of my new clothes. After my weight loss, I had delighted in buying silk and gauzy cotton blouses, tailored pants, drapey skirts. I fancied pink, daring patterns, and striking sandals and boots.

For my date with Stuart I chose blue jeans and a pink silk top. I felt I was taking myself along as a separate person. My life had been rich in social experiences, but this was as far from the usual dinner party as my garden was from a minefield.

The Indian restaurant owner shook my hand enthusiastically as I came through the door. "How are you tonight? It's nice to see you again. Where would you like to sit?" I had wanted a few minutes to scope the place out to identify Stuart, but the owner was grasping my elbow excitedly, waiting to escort me to the table of my choice. I was as nervous as a seventh grader. What if I went up to the wrong man?

A furtive look around revealed only one single man in the restaurant, sitting primly at a table by the window in suit and tie. It looked to me like he was strenuously pulling in his stomach. I told the restaurant owner I was meeting a friend, feigned confidence, and walked over to the man I prayed was Stuart. He smiled and stood up as our eyes met; we shook hands, and he pulled out my chair. His cologne would have overwhelmed a musk ox.

Stuart was a psychotherapist. Listening was his specialty, and eliciting personal information his talent. Over a plate of mixed hors d'oeuvres, he asked me about my marriages, and I told him about the time my first husband, Ernest, came at me with a kitchen knife, a vacant look in his eyes that I will never forget, and how I thought he would kill me—how I slid calmly away along the kitchen counter and out of the house, leaving him alone with the children.

"What a frightening experience," Stuart said, leaning toward me on his elbows. "You did just the right thing in leaving."

"You think so?" Why was I telling this story on a first date? An hour of free psychological counseling would not propel us into bed, but I was stuck in a conversational groove. "I figured it wouldn't do the kids any good to have me dead, and I really thought I might be dead if I stayed there."

The waiter arrived with the main course and fussed over how to fit the remaining hors d'oeuvres, the candle, the rice, the eggplant korma, the chicken, the spinach, the enormous puff of a puri, and the side of chutney onto the small glass-topped table.

After everything was in place, Stuart squinted in sympathy and slowly shook his head. "Are your kids all right now?"

I served myself and put a spoonful of eggplant on Stuart's plate as well. "Do you want some chutney?"

"Oh, indeed."

It felt familiar and comforting to play the feminine role I had been brought up to play—the man makes the date and pulls out your chair, and you handle food. I ladled chutney onto his plate, then helped myself to the chicken and spinach and broke off a large piece of the puri. "Yeah. I guess they're okay. It's hard to know what goes on under the surface, but I think they're okay."

"Sometimes people suffer from what they call post-traumatic stress disorder when things like this happen. How long ago was it?"

"Fifteen years, maybe."

"Oh well, you're probably all fine by now. I can tell you are —you look fine to me." He reached across the table and gave my hand a little squeeze, then took a bite of chicken kofta. "Where is your ex-husband now?"

"He is dying of cancer in the Bronx."

"Oh. You've had such a hard time." Stuart shook his head again, as if this were one of the most heart-rending tales he had ever heard.

"I feel strange telling you all these things. I barely know you."

"Don't give it a second thought. You're a very interesting woman. We all have stories."

"What's yours?"

"Just some romantic disappointments, things like that, a divorce." His refusal to share his story with me, as I had shared mine, felt manipulative. So far, he wasn't much fun, but then I wasn't being much fun either. I scooped up sauce with my puri, pondering whether this would be our last date. I fought my impulse to reject him instantly. Maybe in the past I had rejected men I would have enjoyed if only I had given them time to get around to their own story.

The waiter cleared the table, and as we waited for the honeyballs, Stuart reached across and took my hands in his again, studying them carefully. I was glad I had refreshed my nail polish. "You're lovely."

He paid for dinner, though I offered to split it. This sure was a traditional date.

"How would you like to go to the opera some time?" he asked as we stood on the street corner, about to go to our cars.

"That would be really nice. What kind of operas do you like?"

"Mostly Italian. Puccini, Verdi."

"So do I."

"Are you free next week?"

Stuart was offering to take me to the opera! I had a moment of panic as I realized that I wouldn't be free for at least four weeks. I had crammed my life with interesting things to do, but it smacked me on that street corner—I would have to make room for dating. "I know this sounds silly, but I work and go to school at night during the week, and I already have plans every weekend until next month."

"Oh. Okay. Well, I'll give you a call." He hugged me and kissed my cheek fervently, leaving a patina of cologne on my skin. I doubted we'd ever see each other again. I knew I wouldn't call him—he wasn't interesting enough—and to him, my story about my busy schedule had probably sounded preposterous.

Still, Stuart had touched me and kissed my cheek, and he had asked me out again. I began to calm down. I could do this.

· 9 ·

My Turn to Do Something

Men were not going to fall out of the sky. There were only a couple of dozen eligible men on the classical music lovers site, so I widened my search to Yahoo!, Match.com, and American Singles and emerged into a world where there were thousands of "men seeking women."

Yahoo!'s dating site is free at the basic level, so I signed up and read dozens of profiles. The first man to contact me was a forty-one-year-old, rugged, mustachioed, shirtless hunk of a fireman from California. *Let's get together*, he wrote.

You're gorgeous, but how I can get together with someone in California?

It's easy. He offered cybersex.

I don't think it would be interesting to have sex with thin air, I answered, and that encounter ended.

I kept reading. I learned men's religion and age, their marital status, living situation, and income. They chose their favorite movie and place for a honeymoon or first date. I knew their height, body type, and hobbies, and I looked at their photographs.

In 2003, creating an Internet profile was a new concept. Nobody I knew had done it; even computer nerds. I worked on a computer at my job, but this was a different part of the technological forest. The steps were outlandish: a member name, a screen name, a password, an anonymous e-mail address, and so on. I was guided through the profile:

age (60)
height (5'9")
weight (145)
body type (slender)
where I live (Montclair, New Jersey)
profession (legal secretary)
education level (two MAs)
religion (other)
children (have children who don't live with me; don't
   want any more children)
income level ($50,000-$75,000)
what I'm looking for (a man between fifty and sixty-five
   —"sixty to seventy-five" sounded just too old)
sports (swim 30 laps a day)
hobbies (I play the piano and sing)

With Stuart, I had given up on sending a photograph through e-mail, but if I was going to proceed with my project, I had to figure it out—so I turned to the IT department at work. They showed me how to scan a sporty picture of me in blue jeans and a white T-shirt with a red bandanna around my head. I twisted my mind into a new world where I spent my days with total strangers who might be necrophiliacs or my next love.

If I hadn't been scrolling through profile after profile and firing off e-mails from my secretarial station, I would have been more diligent about filing papers or reorganizing my desk. I had been working for the same attorney for ten years and hoped my record of reliable efficiency would discourage him from firing me because of my transient insanity. God knows the lawyers in the firm suffered from various forms of insanity themselves. Chuck used to show up bare-chested and sweaty in his tiny little running shorts, and he had his secretary order his porn films and make dates for him. A real estate attorney named Mike had such a loud mouth and vile tongue that people often shut his door as they passed his corner office. My own obsessions would probably go unnoticed.

At night I sometimes forgot to eat dinner as I corresponded with one set of men while reading about others. It was a mad fever. As each e-mail or instant message popped up on the screen, I felt I was being almost physically touched. Even boring men were interesting because there were so many of them, each boring in a different way.

I would have been more comfortable meeting a man the old-fashioned way, so a friend and I tried a hotel bar, hoping for at least a conversation with a traveling salesman, but we felt foolish—and I guess that showed, because nobody spoke to us. I had grown up in a world where a girl would *never* have asked a man out, except on Sadie Hawkins Day or for the Girls' Club Dance. It felt strange being an Internet aggressor, contacting one man after another. The men seemed to enjoy it, though, and I wondered why I had waited so long to try this gambit.

In the world of 2003 there was only the illusion of places ripe for meeting the old-fashioned way. The Rowe weekend, the writing group at the library, church, volleyball night at the YMCA, classes at adult school, and book clubs were filled with women following the advice in magazines about the new dating scene. "Go someplace you enjoy." "Just get out of the house—go to the local library or adult school." I guess men didn't read articles in *Cosmopolitan* or *Psychology Today*, because if a man wanted to meet women, he'd find the local library or adult school packed with them. When my son complained he wasn't meeting women, I told him to go to any old dance class—zumba, swing dancing, Highland dancing—they were all full of women. But other than bars, drag races, and Iron Man training camps, where were the men?

But . . . if it was so easy for men to find a date, why were so many men looking for women on the dating sites? Maybe men's lot was not so easy after all. They were endearing as they laid out their dreams on the Internet, specifying various terms of engagement (discreet, casual, long-term) in varying settings (in a boat, by the fire, on a beach, at a candlelight supper). They offered flowers, attention, fun, love, commitment, honesty, humor, appreciation, and sex. Most men found themselves good-looking, honest, and funny. They wrote that, yes, they wanted sex, but also fun, honesty, sincerity, intimacy, and romance. Men lost their mystique as I learned that they, too, were dreaming of laughter and loving arms. They sounded just like women.

My investigations took me to the erotic sites too. I told one New Jersey doctor that he had a most attractive dick, but I didn't go out with men who introduced themselves by sending me pictures of their penis. He replied by sending me a head shot—of his face, that is—making it all the easier to identify him if I should bump into him in the emergency room.

The sheer repetition of no-holds-barred sexual requests—

picture after picture, person after person, couple after couple—
made all kinds of sexual appetites feel normal and acceptable.
There were more ways of getting a penis into a vagina, or
something else into something else, than I had ever imagined.

A seventy-two-year-old widower from rural Georgia sent
me an instant message proposing that we *meet halfway and have
some fun.* I was at work, and my friend, Sybil, who was passing
by my desk, asked me, "What're you smiling at?"

"You won't believe this guy," I said, and read her his
message.

She came around to my side of the desk to watch the
show. Internet dating was brand new and she had never seen
an on-screen interaction before. After IM'ing for five minutes
more, he abruptly wrote, *DO YOU BELIEVE IN INTIMACY
BEFORE MARRIAGE?!?!?*

Sybil said to the screen, "Sex is good, honey. Grow up."

"Poor thing," I said. I imagined him sitting alone in the
house he had shared with his wife, desperate for—what was he
desperate for? The sound of a woman's voice, her touch, a
woman's panties in the hamper, breakfast on the table, sharing
the day's news, and some kind of affection? He had been taught
that the world was black and white, and now he was drowning
in gray.

Though Sybil and I laughed, it was depressing. Maybe only
weirdos and desperados were on the Internet. But, I thought,
I'm on the Internet. There must be other fairly normal people
like me who were there too.

· 10 ·

Finally, a Live One

After a couple of weeks of Yahoo! membership, Bruce e-mailed me:

you're so pretty—adventurous and fun—i'm 54, good-looking, adventurous—little shorter than you—is it ok?

His writing style, without capital letters, was hip and efficient, like e e cummings. His screen name was "gawains-cousinsdad." My literary self was tickled at his play on the name of a knight in an old English tale. He was fifty-four, six years younger than me, but I had been honest on my own profile, so the choice to go out with an older woman was his. He was divorced, lived alone, hair a little gray, liked dancing, movies, theater, playing music and sports, had kids. There was no picture.

I decided to answer him:

God has not seen fit to send me men who are taller than I am. Many things are more important.

After I pushed the "Send" button, I kicked myself for mentioning God. I meant it as a light joke, but he might think I was pious, or sacrilegious, depending on his own view of the world.

He replied that I was the first woman who got it about his screen name.

Oh, I burbled to myself, *he truly appreciates me; he understands that I'm adventurous, and he isn't put off by my advanced education.* I sent him a ratatouille of my further accomplishments, and asked for his photo. Within a half an hour, I had photos of him at the seashore *a few years ago*, in a bathing suit, holding a fishing rod, and a *recent* one of a relaxed, good-looking man with a nice smile. I liked the artwork on the wall behind him. After supporting two husbands, I had a requirement that the men I went out with be solvent, and the photos suggested that he was more than merely solvent.

He was reluctant to reveal anything about himself except that he worked long hours, including some weekends, and valued education. After a dozen or so e-mails, he had still not told me his profession, but I had worked around enough attorneys in my years as a legal secretary to recognize his schedule and his way of writing and conclude that he was a lawyer.

When, as I filed, typed, or answered my boss's telephone, a message from Bruce would pop up on the blue bar at the bottom of my computer screen, I had to force myself not to answer right away, though I was white-hot. I spent hours every day e-mailing him from work and home.

I wondered how, if he was an attorney, he could spend the

same amount of time writing e-mails as I did, though his e-mails were shorter than mine. People are always coming in and out of attorneys' offices—guys from the mailroom, other attorneys, a secretary, the office manager. He could position his computer monitor so that others would not see it, and close it out if someone came in, but it was risky. As he concentrated on seducing me, he might miss a quiet entry into his office.

In the evening after work, I turned off the lights in the living room, put on CDs—Brazilian, bluegrass, Dylan, Marian McPartland, African—and danced my energy out. Through the picture window in my living room I could see the necklace of New York lights lying on the horizon, and that was where Bruce was. New York's energy and drive matched my own, and inside me swirled Bruce, the big city, and my own painful, incurable, unrelenting abandon.

After almost three weeks of daily e-mails, I objected to Bruce that he knew my full name and where I worked, but I didn't know the same about him. He reassured me:

don't stop, big girl,—don't be afraid. I won't hurt you.

I answered:

Of course I'm cautious. I don't know who you are. You could be writing billets doux to a dozen women. You could have genital warts. You could suffer from Narcissistic Personality Disorder. You could live in California.

He wrote back:

i'm wondering how to rank those in order of badness. I think living in calif. is probably the worst.

His teasing made me assert myself, which in turn seemed to amuse and arouse him. When he didn't propose a meeting, and didn't respond when I proposed one, I was confused. If he found me as attractive as he said, and if he really was not in a relationship, why wouldn't he want to meet me?

Jumping into the Fire

hile in this flammable condition, I was asked by my church to be one of the teachers of a sexual education unit for young teenagers. Would I, in other words, like to jump into the blazing bonfire and dance around in it for two hours a week? I said yes.

My fellow teachers were Brad, a congenial, married ex-Marine, and Marcy, a volatile divorcee whose husband had left her for another woman two years before. We took a daylong training course together, but we all felt inadequate to the task. All we knew about sex was what we had personally experienced. None of us had been through a sex education course of any kind. Much of my knowledge about sex came from a series of books, the first of which was *The Happy Hooker*, written in the 1970s by a prostitute named Xaviera Hollander.

"We're the blind leading the blind," said Marcy.

The first unit of the curriculum called for an icebreaker. Brad divided the class into two teams, the boys on one side, the girls on the other, each with an easel and a pen. "You have five minutes to write down as many words as you can for 'penis.'"

The girls scribbled away: *shlong, dick, prick, wee-wee, phallus, johnson . . .*" The words smacked into me with almost physical force. I wanted to leave the room just to catch my breath, but I couldn't, I was the teacher.

The boys raucously outdid the girls: *one-eyed trouser snake, banana, gun, tool, unit, sausage, shaft . . .*

By the end of the contest, I had crossed into giggles with everybody else.

We three teachers knew that our class of thirteen-year-olds would soon enter into a world that couldn't be explained or predicted. Some of them would probably be gay; all would run into excruciating disappointments and tricky situations; they would be delighted, shocked, surprised, and disgusted as their sexual futures opened up. How could we prepare them for the wonders and oddities they would trip over? We'd have to do our best, resigned to the impossibility of our task. How I wished I had had such a class when I was a teenager.

Besides biology we discussed dating etiquette, the purpose of marriage, how to say no, and various moral questions. They learned about sexual practices like anal sex and cross-dressing, which had slammed into me when I was least prepared to deal with them. One evening three gay people, one man and two women, came and talked about their experiences. None of the three had had sex until their mid-thirties because they had been confused. The man said that through his twenties he had thought he was the only man in the world attracted to other men.

Unit 6 featured tasteful drawings of various kinds of sex. One chalk drawing showed an older woman, her long, white hair loose, her head on the shoulder of a man lying next to her in bed. They embraced, smiling.

"Yuck," said Nicky, scrunching his face up in disgust. "That could be my grandparents."

"Come on, Nicky," I said. "Anybody their age has lost a lot in their lives. Why would you deny them the comfort of affection and sex?"

Nicky's face softened. "I never thought about it that way."

The photo of the older couple gave Nicky a view of life that stretched far beyond his randy teenage sexuality. When he grew up, he would know that there did not have to be a finish line for sex. I didn't inform him that I was the age of his grandparents, even older perhaps, and was just as randy and out of control as he was.

I had avoided sexual references, imagery, contact for twelve years. Now I was talking about sex for two hours a week. It took planning and effort, but I acted calm in our basement classroom.

We ended the class with the Condom Olympics. The kids went from station to station, blowing up condoms like balloons, twisting them into rabbit forms, putting them under water—getting a sense of how much pressure condoms could withstand without breaking. They preferred the cherry flavored ones.

· 12 ·

Bruce the Cat

When I signed up for Yahoo!, Match.com, and other dating sites, I was optimistic about finding someone to date, but a couple of months into my project I was stuck, transfixed, in a virtual relationship with Bruce. Lenny's dance and the kisses on the cheek from Michael and Stuart remained my only blossoms. Books, movies, banter —my mother had said quite clearly that men are crazy for sex, but I was now the burning one. Was the men-are-crazy-for-sex story wrong, or was there something wrong with me? I did not want to depend on my own experience for wisdom, even if my sexual history seemed "normal." A honeymoon period, then sex a couple of times a week, then lessening libido because of exhaustion, presence of children, and the corrupting interference of unresolved disagreements and resentments. The unique endgames fatal to each marriage did not seem relevant.

I had to forge ahead, though my confusion was deepening.

Bruce and I assumed roles in our e-mails. For a while he was *daddy*, wanting to read to me as I went to sleep. I joked that I would be *bo peep*, and he addressed me as *bo* for a while. One day he called me *a good man*. That felt uncomfortable, and I jacked myself up:

Are you playing mind games with me?

He answered:

maybe i'm getting carried away. are you afraid that reality can have a very crashing effect?

I wrote back:

If it does, better to crash and get it over with.

Bruce was taking up a lot of my time, and if it wasn't going to lead anywhere, I would have to find another man. I reluctantly, petulantly, tiredly prepared to swallow the "crash" he was warning me about. He wasn't giving me what I wanted anyway.

Bruce's next e-mail proposed that we meet in an hour, and informed me that out of the thirteen million or so people in the New York Metropolitan area, the two of us used the same elevator bank to get to our offices. I had an instant of panic when I wondered if he was someone in my own law firm who had sent me false photographs, but he included the link to his law firm's website and I learned he was a partner in one of the two law firms, his and mine, on my elevator bank. A remark in one of his e-mails, *you are burning up the elevators*, had puzzled me, but was now clear. I "burned" past his office several times a day.

I did everything except think. I didn't even pose a few "what-ifs" to myself. I was ready to tumble down the rabbit hole, and an hour later I walked into his law firm.

The receptionist paged him as I absorbed a portrait of an old man taken maybe in the 1950s, a painting of a sailboat, copies of *Architectural Digest* and *People*, and brochures of the firm, with a picture of Bruce on page three.

Ten minutes later, he came brusquely around the corner. He was an inch shorter than advertised, and five to ten years older than the "recent" picture, but he radiated power and poise, and for that moment I put myself in his care. Being already at the bottom of the rabbit hole, what else could I do?

I stood up, we shook hands with a formal "Good afternoon," and I followed him, client-like, into the conference room.

He shut the door, and stood with his back against it. "So. How about this!" He smiled an excited, conspiratorial smile and pulled me towards him.

"I was so shocked," I said into his neck. "Imagine sharing the same elevator bank! You were really holding out on me."

He held me for a while, running his hands along my body, kissing my neck hungrily. It was like a passionate scene in those romantic movies I had been avoiding for twelve years.

He stepped back mid-grope, drew a chair out from the shiny, oval, conference room table, motioned for me to sit down, then pulled out a chair for himself on the other side of the table and sat sideways with his right ankle folded up to his left knee, his right arm resting comfortably on the table.

"What an adventure this has been." He smiled, suddenly cool as a cucumber.

I smiled, noting that he was speaking in the past perfect tense, the "perfect" part being an indication that something has begun and ended. "And now that we've met?"

"I'm going to Miami this afternoon, have a closing there."

"When will you be back?"

"I'm not sure."

I was disoriented, confused, disappointed, afraid, annoyed, angry, affronted, and a lot of other adjectives. What were we talking about here? I became cool as my own kind of cucumber and sat back casually. "Oh. What kind of closing is it?"

He rolled his eyes. "Difficult. A very difficult one."

"The nice thing about closings is that when they're over, they're over." I hoped I was concealing my anger. He had manipulated me to his office (with my full cooperation), and now he thought he could manipulate me back upstairs with a snap of his tongue.

"You know a little bit about those things, I guess."

I was trying to maintain a bit of poise and grace. "I used to work for a real estate attorney."

"You work at Davies & McGowan, right?"

"Yes."

"As a legal secretary," he confirmed.

"Yes."

This conversation was going nowhere, so I stood up. So did he. He reached out and shook my hand. "It was wonderful meeting you." He opened the door and stood back to usher me out of the conference room with a courteous wave of his hand. He got in the down elevator.

Fortunately, I was alone in the up elevator. I looked at my image in the reflective elevator doors. It showed a woman wearing pants that fit too loosely, a multicolored vest, and a white shirt. She was mannish. If I had known I was going to meet him that day, I would have worn different clothes. I was sure that he had been disappointed. I kicked the elevator door. Why hadn't I said, "I'd love to meet you, but today isn't convenient. How about lunch tomorrow?" He would have said, "I'll be out of town tomorrow." So I would have said, "Okay. Some time next week?" And he would have said, "Sure. That would be great." Running down there like an overeager schoolgirl had been the wrong move, and I couldn't take it back.

Bruce had toyed with me the way my cat, Oscar, toyed with mice. I was a tiny, skittish creature, inexperienced in the pitfalls of Internet romance. Oscar brings his mice onto my porch to dispose of them. Bruce brought me to a conference room in his office.

When I got back home that night, the house felt empty and lonely. I looked out my living room window at the lights of New York. Walking along the streets between the buildings brightly outlined against the night sky were thousands of men who were looking for the same things I was. I could see their apartment lights from where I stood in my darkened living room. Was it possible that every last one of them had a deal-breaking defect? Out of the thousands, all I needed was one. How would I ever find him? Seeing the men on the Internet had raised my hopes, but it, too, felt like a dead end now.

I put on some CDs—Cesaria Evora, Bob Dylan, Diana Krall—and danced around my living room.

Bruce sent me two short e-mails over the next couple of days:

still in closing
hope you're well. this thing is never ending. i'm exhausted.

One lesson I was learning was that it is best to shut up sometimes, so I didn't answer him.

The Internet is a feral kingdom. Dog-eat-dog. Bruce played the game ferociously, shamelessly, and others would, too. My skin thickened up.

The following Monday he wrote me a cryptic e-mail.

i found you intriguing but it couldn't be sustained, especially since i knew who you were in advance.

Months later we had a brief e-mail exchange over a chance business matter involving our respective law firms, and he wrote:

> *i couldn't continue because i had to get back to work. wasn't it fun!*

No.

I set out to meet men, and also to learn about dating, about men, about sex. I knew I would sometimes misjudge a person or a situation and act inappropriately, and that is just what I had done.

I had progressed from a single dance to platonic dates to a kiss on the cheek and now to passionately making out in a conference room. What would be next?

· 13 ·

Strategy

I licked my wounds and regained some of my composure after Bruce's humiliating dismissal. When I looked again at Yahoo! a week later there was a flood of e-mails, twenty or thirty at least. I now had to graduate from helpless mouse to hunter.

Since a man looking for a date would see only my profile, I played with it. If I mentioned all of my virtues—my travel, my many languages, my advanced education—I might appear overqualified for the simple pleasures that most men said they were looking for.

I made a list of qualities I could live either with or without:

INDISPENSABLE	PRO	CON
Solvent	Kind	Mentally unstable
Sane	Intelligent	Addicted
	Sophisticated	Suffering from a
	Liberal-minded	condition that
	Funny	would require
		nursing

Michael was brilliant, but obsessive and out of tune emotionally. Bruce had seemed sophisticated and was probably intelligent, but he was not kind. It was a rare man whose profile didn't announce that he was very funny, but all that mattered was whether I thought so, and I usually didn't think so. A common interest in music, literature, or language might be nice, but I didn't want someone who would compete in my territory. I'd like someone attractive, but there were pictures of gorgeous men on the Internet who didn't appeal to me at all; perhaps they were wearing all white on a fishing boat in Florida, or they postured, like the bare-chested California fireman. Every quality had qualifications and exceptions. Given solvency and sanity, I wanted someone I could feel comfortable with.

My profile should be breezy, light, and disarmingly frank. My attitude toward life and dating should show through. The rest was chemistry.

If I were 100 percent frank, it would read like this:

No sex for twelve years, which is driving me crazy. Want someone who will be a great friend and regular lover. The idea of marriage gives me hives because my two marriages were miserable and ended in difficult divorces.

Hah! What a losing profile that would be!
I experimented with three different profiles; the one on

Yahoo! emphasized my athleticism, the one on American Singles mentioned my piano playing and singing, and the one on Match.com portrayed me as hip and fun-loving.

The responses were more substantial. I walked in a park near my home with a pleasant but unexciting computer scientist from San Francisco, and had coffee in Grand Central Station with a boor of a traffic court judge who walked out on me mid-cup. I had failed to sit in wide-eyed awe as he told me that a small group of conspirators was controlling the United Nations, the Supreme Court, Congress, Russia, China, and the President. I think he suspected I was a Democrat.

Then an e-mail popped up from a man named Ken offering great food, drink, conversation, and of course great sex. He was younger than I and had found that making love with older women was hot because they knew what they wanted. *If your intrested we can take it from there.*

The writing style wasn't polished, his capitalization policy was inconsistent, and he misspelled "you're interested" (Bruce, the hotshot partner in a New York law firm, had spelled "interesting" intresting), but he got to me because in profile after profile men wrote that they didn't want to play games. Here was a man who acted that way.

The blurred photograph showed a round-faced man with wavy brown hair, looking a little stunned but attractive. His profile said he was 35, 6'2", 210 pounds, brown hair, brown eyes, and lived in a town a half hour away.

My work buddy Sybil dismissed Ken as suffering from Oedipal neurosis, but to me he seemed sure-handed, a little humorous, and honest. I answered with a lukewarm e-mail asking for more information, and he replied that he was *looking for a friend who wants to go out and do things, but also wants to get laid from time to time, hey everyone loves getting laid right!* He reassured me further by revealing that he was a cop, *so I wouldn't worry about me hurting you in any way* and asked for my phone number so we could talk more.

He wasn't beating around the bush, and I shouldn't either.

> *A cop! Wow. Never been out with a cop. I don't know if I go along with your logic that since you're a cop you wouldn't hurt me. If you're a cop you could REALLY hurt me, you could find me if I were trying to hide, shoot me with your service revolver, and at your trial your fellow cops would tell everyone what a great guy you are. I'm only joking, well partly joking. It's just that being a cop is a two-edged sword. I was thinking you sounded like a thoughtful guy though, and a frank person who doesn't pull his punches.*

I gave him my phone number, and he called. It was Wednesday when we first spoke. The following weekend he had a police department pig roast, then he was on duty. We made a date to meet eight days later, the following Thursday. He offered to come to Montclair, and I suggested we meet at South Park, the bar where Michael and I had danced. It was next door to my church, where I would have choir practice until 9 p.m.

In the days leading up to Thursday, the hurt from Bruce stung a bit more sharply. I prepared myself for disappointment if Ken called it off, or if we didn't like each other, but I never considered calling it off myself.

There is always a price for sexual satisfaction. According to my father, fast women lost the respect of others. My mother suggested that I would have to be subservient to the animal nature of men. When I was younger, I suffered constant worry about pregnancy, but that worry was gone now. I did not want to cook for anyone, or sew on his buttons, or be constantly available. I didn't want to sacrifice my hard-won peace of mind and independence. I didn't even know if I wanted to go out for "great food and drink" with Ken, as he had proposed. I didn't want to run into acquaintances while out with him. I didn't want to explain him or lie *about* him, and I didn't want to lie *to* him either. I planned to continue my online correspondences, and to date other men.

I managed my own finances, relationships, and schedule (outside of work). I could play the music I wanted, and watch a stupid television show without someone saying, "What are you watching *that* stupid show for?" I ate, slept, and went out as I pleased. The only uncomfortable part of my life, outside of a marginal worry about money, was that I was a little lonely, and starved for sex. Having a friend with benefits might remedy both of those things. Not having a friend with benefits was also taking a toll on me, so it was worth a try. It was sex at a bargain price.

· 14 ·

Miles Away from Church

Thursday evening I left the choir loft and sauntered the thirty yards to the corner of Church and South Park Streets. I didn't want to walk too fast or too slowly. Songs I had never heard before boomed from inside the bar. Women were posturing in skirts that required extensive bikini waxing to wear. Men nursed their beers.

When I was young we drank coffee, not beer, at the Café Figaro in Greenwich Village—or, when I was living in Greece, at the cafés on Kolonaki Square in Athens. They were open, public places, and if you waited long enough, a friend or acquaintance was bound to pass by, or you'd start up a conversation with the people next to you. Inside South Park there was a different atmosphere—brash, overtly sexual, dark, loud.

Ken arrived a few minutes late, looking just like his picture. His leather jacket lay appealingly on his broad shoulders. He opened the door for me, placed his hand protectively against my back as we entered the bar, then pleased me by saying, "Jesus, this is loud. Let's go to the back."

I followed him to the very last booth in the back room. The outside wall was all windows giving onto the sidewalk, leaving me visible to people passing by, including, perhaps, the other choir members on their way home. I felt like a mannequin in a department store window, but I told myself that I wasn't doing anything wrong, so I should calm down. We slid into opposite sides of the booth.

The Goth waitress had black fingernails and lipstick, and her intricately patterned black stockings made her look like she had a terrible skin disease.

"What can I get you? Are you hungry?" Ken asked.

"No, not hungry, thanks. A beer would be great."

"What do you drink?" asked Ms. Goth amiably.

"If you have Stella Artois on tap that would be nice, otherwise Heineken."

She nodded. "Stella Artois."

"I'm going to try this Stella Artois with you. Never had it."

The waitress gave us a mysterious, black-lipped smile and left to get our beers.

"There was traffic on Route 46," Ken began, with a little squirm of frustration.

"You weren't late though, maybe five minutes."

"I felt like I was going to be late. I hate to be late."

"I was at my church next door so it would have been hard for me to be late."

"Yeah? What church?"

"Unitarian."

"Are you religious?"

"I guess. I go to church every Sunday, usually."

"I was raised an Evangelical, and I've had enough of that stuff." He showed no disdain. His style, in e-mails and in person, was matter-of-fact, honest, and non-confrontational.

"I was raised a Christian Scientist and that made me avoid churches for a long time. But I like this one."

We chatted about our families and nursed our beers. I was trying to formulate a strategy—which question would I ask him next? What did I really need to know? He was growing more attractive by the moment—confident, open, and easygoing. My project for the evening was not going to be how to get rid of him gracefully, but how to indicate gracefully that I liked him.

"You got kids?" he asked.

"Two."

"How old are they?" He looked at me for a second, then laughed. "I'm not trying to trap you into telling me how old you are because I already know how old you are. Sixty, right?"

"Right. What about you?"

"Nah, I don't have any kids. Never been married."

"Why didn't you ever marry?"

"I never found the right person. You know how it is. I came close a couple of times. You're not married now, are you?"

"No. I was married twice. Divorced twice. My last divorce was twelve years ago." The actual divorce didn't happen for a few years, but I wasn't going to go into all those details now. Ken only needed to know I had been free for a long time.

I was learning how to shut up.

"So now you decided to start dating again?"

"I began to get tired of the single life." If I had been as blunt as he was, I might have said, "I was dying for sex and that was making me strange."

"I'll bet you weren't expecting somebody thirty-five to go out with"—he made an exaggerated STOP gesture, his palm facing me—"though I've got a birthday in two weeks. So let's say thirty-six."

"Oh goody. You'll only be twenty-four years younger than I am."

He laughed.

"So tell me, why did you want to go out with an older woman?"

He turned his head away to compose his answer. "Older women aren't silly about makeup, hair, that kind of stuff. And you guys know what you want."

"You've been out with other older women?"

"Well yeah"—he softened what he was about to say with a smile and a little laugh—"but you're way above the radar."

I liked his candor. He liked my burst of laughter. "This is going to be an adventure," I said.

When he got up from the table to go to the men's room, I watched him walk. His blue jeans wrinkled over his square, strong buns and thighs. He walked with a slight swagger, slight. On the football field, he would have been a guard or a tackle—solid, strong, tending toward overweight if he was not careful. He turned his head and smiled at me as he went around the corner. Twelve years of celibacy were going to come to an end.

He slid back into the red banquette, took my hands in his, and looked straight at me. "We've gotten to know each other a little. What do you think?"

"I think . . ." (This was such a big step.), "I think the next time you call, I'll invite you to my house. I'll open the door and we'll see what happens."

"Really?" He closed his lips in a smile and paused a moment. "I'm free Wednesday."

"So am I."

His fingers were massaging my hands. "You know, if we go ahead with this we will get to know each other intimately. We'll touch each other everywhere, hold each other. You know that."

"I understand that."

We walked the two minutes to my car in the church parking lot, and I started to panic. It was eleven o'clock at night but I could find myself introducing Ken to one of the tenors in the choir, or maybe the Chairwoman of the Caring Committee coming out of a late meeting. I didn't want to blow this nicely developing encounter, so I dismissed my anxieties. Ken had shown that he knew what he wanted and how to get it, so I let him handle it.

He kissed me lightly on the lips, tapped my bottom, and said, "See you Wednesday." Perfect. His lips felt clean and friendly. It was nothing more than a hint of contact, but the evening would have felt unfinished if there had been no kiss at all. He had done just the right thing, and I liked him even more now.

Wednesday was six days away, enough time to get rattled, and I was a little nervous. Was sex like riding a bicycle?

· 15 ·

Red Silk

Ken called on Sunday. He told me about the pig roast, then asked, "Will you come to the door naked?"

"I don't think so." This was fun.

"In a bathrobe?"

"I have a nice one. Red. Silk."

"Does it have a belt?"

"Yes."

"Take the belt off."

On Wednesday he arrived at exactly 6 p.m. in his enormous SUV, which took up most of my driveway. When I opened the door, wearing only the unbelted red silk robe, he looked me over and said, "Nice. Very nice."

I had no idea what to do next, but he seemed at ease. He walked into the living room and looked around. "Will you give me a tour of your house?"

"Sure. Would you like a beer?"

"Good idea."

We walked through the dining room into the kitchen, where I gave him the beer; then we stopped in my office and looked at the picture-book backyard. The trees running up the mountainside were turning riotous colors in the autumn afternoon. We detoured into the television room, and came full circle back to the front stairs. He gestured with his left arm, and I started up the stairs.

Like a jerk, I showed him the storage rooms and the guest bedroom before showing him my spacious bedroom with a queen-sized bed and three antique dressers, gold silk drapes, a bedside table, and two long mirrors. It was tidy and uncluttered.

When he drew me close and kissed me, still standing in the doorway, it felt natural and comfortable.

The twelve year drought disappeared—poof!

His scent remained on my pillows for days, and I breathed it in with pleasure and relief after so many years of smelling only myself and my late cat.

For the next nine months, he came over once or twice a week, with phone calls and e-mails in between. He was a great lover: physically big in all his parts, uninhibited, communicative, affectionate, humorous, receptive, spontaneous. We let our time together flow wherever it took us, starting in the living room, the dining room, and the kitchen. We sometimes met during the day, when I worried my Mexican landscapers would show up in the backyard. Usually I heard them coming with their loud machines, but occasionally they snuck up on me. I wondered what they would think if they caught a glimpse of a thirty-six-year-old man entangled with their sixty-year-old client.

Sex with Ken lasted forever, sometimes too long and I began to lose my concentration on the matter at hand. We would have whole conversations while in one position—the installation of a new air conditioner, or the political season.

Massaging him was like kneading a five-pound loaf of bread or playing a Rachmaninoff piece with its impossibly wide chords. No matter how I stretched my fingers, I could never encompass his thighs or shoulders or biceps. His feet were more manageable. "Cops love foot massages," he said, lying back with a sigh as I bent his toes and ran my fingers down the tendons, pinched the back of the ankle, and deeply rubbed the outcroppings on the landscape of his foot.

I remembered that he had written, *you guys know what you want and how to ask for it.* I had the green light to assert myself whenever I figured out what I wanted. And if I could assert my preferences and desires in bed, then asserting myself elsewhere would be easy. It felt like giant steps to me, but Ken easily and good-humoredly complied with my whims. "Do what you need to do," he encouraged. Hey. This was easy. If I felt like dancing to "Maggie's Farm," he'd dance to "Maggie's Farm." I wore a variety of outfits to greet him at the door, and one day I gave him a fashion show, dressing and undressing oh so slowly. He smiled and smiled and smiled. I unearthed no fetishes or unusual desires in myself, but I did like to pause for a massage detour, and he liked my surprises.

We talked, sometimes for hours. We laughed over what would happen if I waltzed up to him when he was hanging out with his fellow cops. The idea was ridiculous. He gestured widely, "I'm not going to take you to the Christmas party and, you know, 'Hey Mom! This is Ann.'" I didn't take him to my parties either. We were far away from each other's worlds both physically and socially. Nobody in his world would ever know about our relationship, and unless the neighbors were paying close attention (which I doubted), nobody in my life knew about him. We were each other's secret and I liked it that way. I could enjoy him without factoring him into any other part of my life. I didn't even tell my best friend Greta. It was simple, fun, uncomplicated, honest, and liberating for me, and I would never have to play nice to his boneheaded Police Chief.

I toyed with the idea of our living together, and bumped up against his music, a combination of hip hop, rap, and other contemporary genres which did not move me at all. Having to listen to that alien music all the time would drive me crazy. His taste in clothes, food, music, entertainment, and everything else was different from mine. One day we were standing at the door making plans for his next visit when he swept his hand, palm outward, across his chest, dipped, and slid, "I can bust a move."

I can do the Charleston, the samba, and the twist, but when I busted my own version of a "move," he doubled over in good-natured laughter.

I reminded myself that the day would come when we would have to let each other go.

·16·

Being a Cop

$\mathcal{I}$ have neither a positive nor a negative opinion of cops. They can be saints; they can be criminals. From all I could see, Ken was a good cop. He had only taken a few college courses and didn't like to read, so he wasn't highly educated, but he was physically strong, honest, decent, lacking in prejudice or hatred, and gifted in figuring out the complicated ethics in sticky situations. He was also a born fixer of things, like my blinds or the stuck kitchen drawer. I was interested to hear about his job, and he talked about it frequently.

"You wouldn't believe who's enforcing the law in this country." He shook his head in something like disgust. He told me how annoying it was when the Pepsi-drinking officer on duty before him always turned over the police car with a sticky steering wheel and food wrappers on the floor. He told me stories of corruption and nepotism, about cops breaking the law—not by killing people or harassing them, but by hiding a piece of evidence or two or shielding other cops. The intrigue over promotions, retirements, and transfers was Machiavellian.

He told me in detail how he got dressed every day—the bulletproof vest, the carrier, the ballistic panels, the girdle between the vest and his belt, tie-downs. I didn't know what these things were; it was enough to realize how complicated the police uniform was. Whatever these things were, they were invisible when on patrol. Around his waist he wore the service belt with the gun, handcuffs, pepper spray, a flashlight, his radio, and an extra pair of handcuffs. The equipment in his car: computer, four different levels of siren, spotlights, notebooks, raincoat, club. He offered to come one day in uniform, and I would have liked that, but I thought the neighbors might see him and become alarmed. Instead, he arrived in sweat pants or blue jeans.

He was matter-of-fact about things that ordinary people wax sentimental about. "Yeah, I know CPR. Once I saved a man's life, but most of them die. I did CPR on this old woman once. After a few minutes I could feel her heart start to beat again and I thought, *Hey, this is cool.* She had choked on a hamburger. They thought they had gotten all of it out, but some of it was still stuck in her throat. She died afterwards. Like I said, most of them die."

I share his approach to things that you can't do anything about: I am unlikely to burst into tears; the emotion lives much deeper down, in the places that last for a lifetime. I still feel pangs about my father's early death in 1966. My brothers are reluctant to talk about him and nobody else could understand the pathos of his loss. I can get frazzled by superficial events more easily than Ken but, like him, I move on quickly from a lost court case, my car being totaled while parked, or other spilt milk.

"Last week I had to take a man down," he told me one afternoon while standing naked by my bed. I was lying on my side, my head propped up on my hand.

"What exactly does that mean?"

"There was this guy going off in an alleyway, right next to some stores. There were some people watching him, and I told them to get away. You never know what they might do. So this guy is screaming and belligerent. He comes toward me and I put my hand out and say, 'Stop.' He grabs my hand! Can you believe that? That is *definitely* not allowed. So I'm thinking this guy isn't going to get talked down. We're going to have to take him out of here, and I reach out and take him like this . . .'"

He bent his knees and stepped to the side, thigh muscles surging like rocks on a mountainside, "and I get him around the neck," he turned as if turning the man around, his arm around his neck, "and boom," he swept his leg swiftly, clipping the legs of the imaginary crazy guy, "he's down." He knelt down on one knee, holding the imaginary man's arms behind his back. "He's kicking and screaming and trying to get away, and then my partner comes and puts the cuffs on him and that's that." He stood up, smiling. "You know, I don't get that way very often. I'm pretty calm, but I think my partner Caprio liked the way I handled that. He'd never seen me do something like that before."

I was spellbound. "You make it look so easy."

"When you know how to do it, it's easy. We see all kinds of stuff. A couple of weeks ago I get a call to check out a car in a school parking lot, and I find this couple having oral sex. So the woman says to me, 'We were just talking,' and I say to her, 'Do you always have a chat with a guy's cock in your mouth?'"

I giggled. "Did you really say that?"

"They kept insisting they weren't doing anything, and I said, 'Okay, here's what we'll do. I'll take you both down to the station and you can tell your story to the guys down there.'

And the guy says, 'You can't do that!' And I say to him, 'Don't worry. Maybe your wife can come and post your bond.' 'I'm not married!' the guy says indignantly. So I say to him, 'If you want them to believe that, you'd better take that ring off your finger.'"

"So what happened?" I couldn't imagine being in such a situation.

"I didn't want to ruin their lives, I just wanted them to get out of there. They pissed me off with their 'Who me!' stuff. But I let them go."

Besides learning about being a policeman, I learned what it was like to come from a blue-collar background. His mother had trouble supporting herself on a modest salary. His father had disappeared long ago. Nobody had Ken's back, and his life would unfold from his own decisions and actions, which left little room for error and stripped away frippery and delusion. Ken was solid as a rock.

· 17 ·

A Nice Jewish Doctor

The stream of e-mails from younger men continued. The most surprising thing was how they "wondered if I would consider" going out with them, as if I were the prize, not they. They didn't view me as desperate and old, but as experienced, smart, and safe.

Ken once patted my mattress and said, "Once you make it this far, age doesn't matter."

Howard described himself on his profile as "a very nice Jewish doctor":

I would make a good father and a pretty decent mother in a pinch. I can change a diaper but not a tire.

His last girlfriend had been sixty-two, twenty years older than he was, and he was still smarting over their breakup. That was at least closer to my age than Ken, who was twenty-four years younger. Like virtually all men, Howard told me his sexual preferences early on—he liked hirsute women. I told him I was not at all hairy, and he remarked, "You can't have everything."

He sent me pictures of himself with the techs in the hospital. In one he was pretending to give CPR to a female nurse lying on a gurney. His fingers were holding her nose closed as he turned earnestly to the camera. The nurse was rosy from laughter.

He sent me pictures of Mariano Rivera, several New York Giants, street signs, lollipops, and balloons of comic characters. His favorite television programs were *Sports Center*, *Old Jews Telling Jokes*, and *South Park*. When we discussed going out on a date, he suggested Coney Island.

We talked on the phone almost every night, and week after week went by with all his free time sucked up by his mother. They lived together in a big, old house near Newark. From his description, she seemed a bitter, nasty woman who sat alone in the house watching television and monitoring her aches and pains. When I asked what it had been like to be raised by her, Howard shot back, "Suffocating." I, too, had sacrificed much of my personal life when I moved in with my sometimes-difficult mother for the last few years of her life, so I could hardly judge him for doing the same.

Two months after our first phone call, Howard finally had a Saturday night off, and I invited him to dinner. We discussed the dinner menu on the phone and I teased, "I think I'll serve you a hot dog and an arugula salad."

"Ann, Ann, Ann, please serve me something I can pronounce."

He got lost on the way to my house, finally arriving in his medium-blue 1998 Honda after several cell phone conversations that guided him to my driveway.

He was tall and slouched. His legs were long and his torso

short, giving the impression of legs topped with ringlets of black hair, graying along the sides. He badly needed a haircut. His high school and college basketball careers were far behind him, and his muscles were lax. His doctor's hands felt soft. He was wearing sweat pants with a spot on them, a sweat shirt, and old sneakers.

After learning about his fondness for umbrella drinks, egg omelettes, Chia Pets, and the 99 Cent Store, I wondered how he would feel in a house decorated with antique American furniture, pewter plates, spatterware, and my grandfather's paintings.

Like Ken, he wanted a tour of my house, and after walking through the first floor he commented, "You have a really nice house, but I think you need a plastic cover on your couch."

Unlike Ken, he continued into the living room, not up the stairs. From there we went into the kitchen, where I served him a mushroom omelet. With the addition of ketchup, he found it very tasty.

He called me "Catholic," and I corrected him. "Howard, I'm not Catholic. I'm Unitarian-Universalist."

"What's the difference?"

"UUs don't have priests, and we don't have the Eucharist, and we don't have a Pope, and we don't have a dogma, and most of us don't believe in Jesus Christ as our savior, and just about everything is different, except that we both meet on Sundays in a church, only sometimes UUs don't call it a church."

He still called me a Catholic. Too much of this sort of thing might be annoying, but I hadn't had too much of anything from Howard yet. He was full of surprises, and amusing.

When we climbed into bed after dinner, he kept up his wisecracks, and it seemed to me that he was nervous. We were not in sync, but this was only the first time we had made love,

I thought. Maybe it would get better as we both relaxed.

I changed the sheets because Ken was coming over the next day. I felt a duty to be shocked at my promiscuity, but my real feeling was delight that my project had finally succeeded beyond my wildest dreams. I wondered why I had always thought that in order to have sex, I would have to surrender my freedom. I was astonished that neither Ken nor Howard was unsettled when I told him I was dating other people too.

A few weeks later, Howard showed up to go to my neighbor's Christmas party wearing sneakers, blue jeans, and a sweatshirt. This was the first time in many years that I had gone to a party with an escort (not counting the disastrous trip to New York with Michael), and I had gotten dressed up in a silk skirt and blouse. At 5'9", I loomed over most men when I wore heels, but I could wear them with Howard. My embarrassment at his dishevelment was tempered by recognition that my expectations were often out-of-date, and in fact my neighbor, who was in her thirties, seemed not to notice at all. Some of the other guests were wearing blue jeans, though there were no other sweatshirts.

When my neighbor's mother found out Howard was a doctor, she changed from jovial to suffering. "Something's wrong with my feet. I've been to so many doctors, and nobody has been able to figure out what's the matter with me. I'm in pain all the time. I don't go out, I just sit at home and hurt."

"What doctors did you go to? Did you see a vascular guy?" he asked.

"Neurologist, orthopedist, internist, rheumatologist, you name it."

"I think you should see a vascular guy. Let me look a minute." He crouched down, his Pepsi in one hand, his free hand feeling along her leg. "I still say you need to go to a vascular guy."

Howard seemed happy to give a lengthy consultation. It

was the compassionate thing to do. I had wanted to get to know Howard outside the medical atmosphere that surrounded him when we talked every night, but maybe, for Howard, medicine was all there was.

My neighbor's mother died of cancer a few months later. Howard shrugged. He was as casual about weighty medical matters as Ken was about weighty police matters.

When we had first corresponded, in September, I'd told him I hadn't had sex in twelve years, and he was proud to claim the mitzvah of breaking my twelve-year sex drought. I didn't have the heart to tell him that by the time he tore himself away from his mother, Ken and I had long been abed.

Our phone calls happened late at night, and without time together to flesh out the relationship, it was boring, and I was always tired the next day, so the phone calls stopped.

· 18 ·

Good-Bye

Ken told me about women he met at parties, in bars, at work, and I told him about men I met or corresponded with. The "with benefits" part of our relationship did not interfere with the transparency and honesty of our friendship.

I asked why he had become a policeman, and he rubbed his thumb against his second and third fingers. "Money."

"But don't you want something besides money, like stimulation or prestige or something?"

"Not really. I just want to have a family and be able to take care of it."

I slid my fingers along his cheek. "So that's why you're seeing someone who's sixty years old?"

He kissed my fingers. "I'll find someone to be my wife someday. I hope soon." He put his hand on my arm. "You understand that, right?"

I patted his shoulder and gave him a kiss on his cheek. "Of course. You'll be a wonderful husband, and a wonderful father."

"Thanks. It feels really good to hear you say that."

I felt sad at the idea of losing him, but I didn't tell him that. I didn't give him my lecture about marriage, either—how inevitable regret is, how disappointments pile on each other, how exhausted both partners become, especially when they have children; how you drop the ball. This smart, loving, self-aware man would be able to make a marriage work without my advice.

The stability he provided made me more carefree with other men. Knowing that I could always have sex made me more calm and sensible. His realistic nature made me relax in the confidence that there would be no desperate good-byes or fruitless longing for the impossible, no operatic professions of love, no regrets, and also that there would be no Ken after a while. The clarity of our understanding made it easier to accept the inevitable.

After we had been seeing each other for about eight months, Ken told me he had run into Elaine, a woman he had dated years before, at a party. He had mentioned before how he regretted having let her slip away. "So this guy, her boyfriend, he says to her, loud, right in front of everybody, 'You're so fucking fat. You're butt-ugly.' And she's not even fat! Not at all! Anyway, I stared at him, and this jerk sticks his face right up to mine and says, 'What the fuck you lookin' at?' So I go real quiet and I say, 'You shouldn't talk to her that way.' And he goes, 'Why don't you mind your own business?'"

I was rapt—my people don't indulge in this sort of Wild West encounter. They seek counseling.

He went on with his story. "'I'm making this my business.' And then this asshole grabs Elaine, twisting her arm, and I step between them. 'You're coming with me,' I say, and I take her right out the door."

"The boyfriend just let you go?" I was straining to visualize this scene.

"People don't mess with cops." He was silent for a while, then he told me, "I wanted to let you know about this because, well, I've told you about Elaine before, right?"

"Yes. I remember."

"I have this funny feeling that she's the woman for me. We've seen each other a couple of times. She's staying with her folks now, but she's got to decide what to do. I don't think she wants to go back to that asshole—god, I hope not." He seemed distressed. "We've talked on the phone every day." He flexed his lips. "I told her I'd help her move out, you know, go with her to get her stuff from their apartment. I hope, I just hope."

When I saw him a week later he sat on the edge of my bed, his head in his hands, "I don't know what I'm going to do. Elaine's gone with her family to Pennsylvania. They've got a summer place on a lake there. I asked her when I'd see her and she said, 'I don't know. I'm so confused.' I tell you, Ann, for the only time in my life I looked at my service revolver and didn't want to live anymore."

"You mean you were contemplating suicide? Really?" Ken's despair was not mine to cure, but he shocked me.

"No. No. I don't think I would have done it. It's just that's how bad I felt. I've never felt that way in my life."

I was lying against the pillows of my bed and he came and sat next to me, taking my hand. "Don't worry. I didn't mean to upset you. I'm not going to kill myself. I just feel like I can tell you these things."

Three weeks later, Elaine came back, and he turned all his attention to her. I missed Ken, but by then he was no longer the only man in my life.

· 19 ·

Don't Do That!!!

had lunch on a spring day with Greta and another friend, Jane. We sat under an umbrella in the back patio of our favorite Italian restaurant on Valley Road in Montclair. Both had been married for decades, and they were good-naturedly envious of my freedom to run rampant in the fields of romance.

A few weeks before, I had met a thirty-seven-year-old businessman named Frank (screen name "funallways"). We began instant messaging on Tuesday, and on Saturday, when I was home from work, he offered to come to my house. I gave him my address.

I gulped after agreeing to his proposal, asked him to give me his last name, and looked him up in the phone book before he came over. I called Greta to tell her what was happening, and to give her Frank's full name and address.

"Don't let him in, Ann!" she exploded. "Ignore the

doorbell. This is crazy. Everybody says that the first rule of blind dating is to meet people in a public place!"

"I know. But I didn't sense any destructive energy in him. He's easygoing and unthreatening."

"The serial killer is always a quiet guy. You can't tell."

"But I wonder," I answered. "A serial killer will put energy and charm into his seduction. He would always bend the conversation toward seduction and doing what he wants. Frank isn't like that at all."

"You're a grown-up. You can do what you want. Just be careful, and call me after he leaves so I know you're still alive."

My assessment proved accurate. Frank blew in the door wearing a big smile (which rarely left his face), a sparkling white T-shirt, pressed khakis, and immaculate white sneakers. He shook hands with me, then stood back, which was a little odd. He told me later that he had a touch of autism, though he had managed to get degrees from Yale and the Wharton School of Business. He credited his mother for ignoring everybody's advice and getting the right education for him.

After that first afternoon, he came over every week or so. He didn't want a serious relationship. He just wanted to "play," and hoped to "retire" soon. He was only thirty-seven and I wondered what he would do after he retired. "Play. Travel." I didn't know how a person could spend decades playing, but he had his plans and was doing what was necessary to accomplish them. He had several successful businesses, and his cell phone rang often as he instructed construction workers, set up meetings, and gave colleagues information. He loved sex, but did not like much physical contact. Sex was brief and to the point, with little foreplay, and no kisses. He liked being tied down, and I tried to comply, but didn't know how to make the proper knots, so they kept coming undone.

One Saturday, an IM from Frank popped up on the screen of my computer at home. We chatted a while, then he wrote,

"Would you like me to come over?" "Sure," I responded. We IM'd at two, he left at four, and we both got on with our days. Not a bad arrangement, though I felt like a bonobo ape. (Bonobo apes have sex all day long, every day, and they live a remarkably peaceful life.) After he left, I was feeling placid. Sex calmed me. I could concentrate easily, and my anxieties were attenuated.

Frank was slight in build. It was like holding a teenager. It was like being fucked by a pogo stick. He had a lot of interesting things to say, but we eventually drifted apart.

OUR LUNCHEON ON THE sunny patio was the first time I saw Greta after meeting Frank, and she was still outraged that I would allow a man to come to my home without knowing anything about him. "You have to be careful! I know it's adventurous and fun and all that, but you have to protect yourself! He could have been anyone!"

Jane laughed. "Better you than me. I don't think I would have the nerve to do that."

There was a lot I was not telling them, such as the gritty details of letting some guys play out their quirks and twists in e-mails to see where it led. If I ever found myself in a reliable, fulfilling relationship, I would not be spending my days corresponding with total strangers about pee fetishes, sado-masochism, and group sex, but this was my chance to learn what was true.

I knew when I began this quest that I risked losing the respect of my employer, friends, and most importantly, my children and the rest of my family. Some people might call my casual sexual relationships with Ken, Howard, and Frank immoral or undignified. The normal, respectable sixty-year-old woman was expected to be quiescent sexually—that is what I had expected myself. It was shocking to find out that libido could flame intensely so late in life. Looking back, I see clues that this happened to some of my female relatives, but it was never allowed to surface in an open conversation.

I didn't know at what point my friends or family would gradually exclude me from dinner parties, holiday celebrations, or other social occasions. So there was a lot that I kept to myself.

Sanity was one of my requirements, but what did that mean? What was normal? I had been led all my life to believe that gentlemanly behavior was normal. Yet some of the seamiest public scandals have involved people who appeared gentlemanly. Scam artists and priest child molesters were courteous and well liked. Senators and preachers who were revered by their constituencies often hid devastating secrets. How could I identify the normal ones? Though I was willing to consider Lenny, the cross-dresser, "normal," I didn't share his sexual proclivities. What proclivities could I tolerate? That was the correct question to ask.

If I wanted to answer those questions, I had to listen and learn, even if it meant hiding this information from my friends and family.

· 20 ·

The Grab Bag

One man published a post, "Sipping a Latte and Have That Urge To Tinkle?" on Craigslist. This made me laugh, so I answered him, asking what a "Golden Shower" was. He explained that some men like women to pee in front of them, or into their mouths. That's what he liked, and he wrote that he had been bothered that others found a pee fetish weird and abnormal, but then he saw people on television *drinking churned up cockroaches and eating live bugs... Pee is STERILE and 99% water...* He assured me that he wasn't a *weirdo* or *freak* and that he *could come to Thanksgiving Dinner with your folks.*

Another man lived "the life," meaning the group sex life. He wondered if I'd like to go to Las Vegas with him to a convention of like-minded people, which he assured me would be *life-changing* and *more fun than you could ever imagine.* I declined.

A banker wrote lyrically about sadomasochistic practices, and married men proposed various kinky arrangements.

All men began their correspondence with bold sexual statements or questions. I was shocked, but also interested in this pattern. The opening gambits were often raunchy and coarse. Malcolm from Glasgow, Scotland began writing me every day:

do you feel my gentle kisses on your vagina, my hands softly caressing you?

If I met Malcolm at a dinner party, he wouldn't be panting over the hors d'oeuvres about putting his hands in my panties and feeling the soft hair underneath. The Internet freed men to express raw desire. Maybe this stream-of-consciousness writing was giving me a window into how men's minds worked. I now had the privilege of seeing what a man might really be thinking over the hors d'oeuvres.

I tried to finesse my way through the opening barrage into true conversation, but in Malcolm's case the true conversation never began. In our third week of correspondence I said I didn't like *sex with thin air*, and he made a counterproposal:

It might be fun for you to lie in a bath and gently caress yourself as we talk.

I wondered what he would say when his wife opened the phone bill and asked about the long call to New Jersey (which never happened) while I was gently caressing myself in the bathtub. These fantasies get tangled up in real-life concerns.

After a while, Malcolm stopped writing. I assumed that he had found someone who loved sex with thin air.

· 21 ·

Sometimes It Really Is Dangerous

was contrite when I responded to Greta's scolding about ignoring safety practices. If she had known about another dangerous episode, she might have graduated from scolding to disgust or disrespect. Frank (one mistake which turned out all right) was different from Hank, who introduced himself by sending me a picture of himself sitting naked on a motorcycle in his living room in Texas. He wasn't lascivious or leering, just a naked, lanky, neatly bearded, balding, handsome sixty-year-old man. There were a couple of other pictures too, showing him clothed, relaxed, and confident in the Amazon jungle, Kazakhstan, Surinam, and Eritrea. His lascivious e-mail was simply a graphic presentation of the thoughts other men presented verbally. All men started with sex; Hank was just bolder about it.

On a lark, I answered the e-mail, and within a couple of days he had started calling me every day. Once I heard that mellifluous Texas baritone, "Hello darlin'," I got more interested. He apologized profusely about the naked picture.

He was an oil rig engineer who worked a few lucrative months a year, going from contract to contract. He wasn't rich but considered himself comfortable, and planned to retire soon. I had not spent a single minute of my life thinking about oil rigs, so everything was new to me. As he told it, there were uncertain sands and rock formations, water spurting up unexpectedly or not at all. Human peculiarities also interfered with getting the oil out of the ground. Every geological formation and drilling site required a different scientific and personal formula. He was defensive about his work, complaining, "People don't understand what's involved in drilling for oil. They think it's so easy."

Whenever he referred to his two ex-wives, the roiling anger in his voice bothered me. According to him, they had robbed him blind and kept him away from his children. I had dropped my resentment and distaste regarding my first husband into a personal black hole which I hoped neither exuded nor absorbed energy. Hank was handling his disappointments differently.

He had stories. "In Moscow you sign in, go up to your room, and a few minutes later there's a prostitute knocking on your door. It was just one of the hotel's services. I never let them in. They're diseased." Or, closer to home, "There was this woman in Houston who was super clean. She always made me take a shower, and she put a plastic sheet on the bed. Then one night she comes out of the shower with a hairnet on her head, and she wants me to wear one too! That was just too much, and I told her, 'Listen, honey, I just can't do this,' and that was that."

He asked me to visit him in Texas, and said he'd return the visit later. I knew very little about Houston, and what I did know didn't interest me much, but every place is interesting if you know somebody there. I said I would fly down.

He planned to pick me up at the airport and drive me to his home an hour away. We'd visit his aunt in Louisiana. We'd go dancing in Beaumont, with me wearing his lizard skin cowboy boots, if they fit me. His son was organizing a "Texas-size barbecue." This was as exotic to me as Surinam or Kazakhstan.

I had traveled to new places alone many times, and met many traveling companions who started out strangers, but this was more than just traveling alone. I was entrusting myself to someone I had never met, without the protection of a hotel to retreat to.

By the time I learned that Hank's house was a converted trailer across from a McDonald's, I had already bought my airline ticket.

Two nights before I was to leave he called to make detailed arrangements for our airport meeting, but he swerved abruptly into politics. "You liberals are trying to bring down all the rich people in America."

I think I laughed. "What do you mean?"

"You don't want anybody to make any money. You just want to keep spending it on things like the Indians. Fuck the Indians. They lost. We build them homes with our tax money and they knock out the windows and fill the bathtubs with water for their horses."

"What?"

"And then somebody comes along who has some balls, who's not a fucking pansy, and everybody hates him. Give me one reason why these people hate George Bush. That man's got balls. At least someone's got balls. Just one reason."

That seemed like a question to me, so I began to answer, "He's a deceiver."

The phone went dead. I was not sure whether to be angry or not. There might have been a good reason for the sudden disconnection, though the timing of the silence at the other end of the line suggested that he had hung up on me. I called him back. The phone rang a few times before he picked it up.

"Did you hang up on me?" I asked.

"Yes, I did."

I pulled in a sharp breath of anger and lowered my voice to almost a whisper. "Some things happen just once in a lifetime, and hanging up on me is one of them."

"Well, here's number two."

I stared at the silent phone in my hand. So much for Texas balls. Give me Yankee ovaries any day.

· 22 ·

Triage

Just like a fifteen-year-old in thrall to her libido, I had made a stupid decision, and felt lucky to have discovered Hank's true nature in time. So I was contrite for more reasons than Greta or Jane knew when I offered my *mea culpa* over Frank. "I know. I was wrong."

"You're a bad girl." Greta sipped her Chablis with a frown. "This time you survived, but the next time you might not."

We chomped on our salads and ate our sandwiches, and after catching up on all that had happened since we had last seen each other the conversation turned back to my adventures, and I told them about the dozens of married men who had contacted me. "Maybe it's the changes I've made to my profile, or the new photo or something, but more and more married men are contacting me."

Greta spoke with certainty. "Don't bother with them. You might get hurt."

"Of course! But married people get hurt all the time. They deal with it themselves and it doesn't escape the marital cocoon. Nobody could ever hurt me as badly as my husbands did."

Jane moved her chair over to get out of the sun. "I don't know if I told you what happened when Bill and I drove out to pick up Bess from college."

"What happened?" I asked. I had given them insight into what I was doing; now Jane was going to tell me what happened inside a successful marriage.

"Bill was in a foul mood. Marriage is some love, some hate, you know, and there was nothing but hate coming from him. He was horrible. So I told him that if he hated me this much, I'd go and stay in the country house, and he could go back to the city. I wasn't going to listen to him rail on and on against me day after day. It took him a couple of hours but he finally apologized. I think he sensed that I was serious, and I was. You know what I think—you have to keep good-bye on the tip of your tongue. Even after forty years of marriage, if he's not treating you right, you've got to leave."

We finished our lunch with a shared bowl of ice cream, and Greta said, "Look what you're learning. I've gone through my whole married life never having these experiences, never learning what you're learning. It may be knowledge that I can live without, but it's interesting."

There was so much to learn. What was my hurry?

I triaged for a lengthening list of deal-breakers: Was he married, or worse, married with children? Was he struggling financially? Was he more than two hours away? Was he bitter? Was he a hard-and-fast Republican? Was he a conservative Christian? A "yes" to any of these questions would disqualify any man. The conservative Christians scared me the most. They were so unaccustomed to acknowledging their potent sexual needs that they fumbled in guilt and confusion. I wondered what kind of encounter would ensue if I met one of them and did not care to find out. They had eagerly gobbled the fairy stories, and when they learned that reality did not conform to their expectations, they didn't know how to behave.

The male animal was becoming demystified. As I dealt with men in my daily life, I was more compassionate. I knew that under their studied veneers lurked secret lives.

I had opened the grab bag, and men came tumbling out. Of course, I didn't need the entire contents of this piñata—I only needed one, or possibly two, and that search was like looking for a unicorn. The alabaster creature gracefully leaps out of the woods into a clearing (my inbox) where you can see it clearly. He looks straight at you with those limpid eyes, and asks you to meet up at the next oak tree. Up close, he's a dun-colored buck feeding on the lowest leaves. You have fleeting thoughts of Lyme disease. But there's that velvet mouth, those well-muscled thighs . . .

· 23 ·

Married Men

The underside of marriage lay exposed on the Internet. Even two marriages and two divorces had not prepared me for what I read there. Married men poured misspelled desire at me. They IM'd, phoned, and e-mailed me from all over. It was exciting, hypnotic. It was also alarming to think of the wives who slept unawares next to these erupting men. Now I was not the Wife, I was the Other Woman.

The men who wrote to me seemed to want a new pattern of desire to disrupt them and dislodge things. I didn't think that their lust had much to do with my irresistible loveliness, but rather everything to do with them.

Antonio contacted me through Match.com in March 2004. His photo showed startling blue eyes, a full head of white hair, and a handsome, youthful face. He worked a few blocks away from me on Park Avenue. We e-mailed a few times and he asked for my phone number. I pressed "Send" on the response, and a few seconds later my phone rang.

Before I could even say "hello," a man's voice said, "Meet me at Starbuck's in ten minutes."

It was ten thirty in the morning, and I couldn't leave my desk for more than a few minutes. After my foolishness with Bruce, some counter-suggestions sprang to mind—"Could we make that lunch?" being one—but the very spontaneity and urgency of his demand was what made it exciting. "Uhh . . ."

"Ten minutes."

Here was John Wayne, Steve McQueen, Clint Eastwood. I said, "Okay." Nobody would ever know if I took fifteen minutes to myself. I had nothing invested in Antonio. I would meet him in a public place, and if he was obnoxious, I'd leave.

On the esplanade outside Starbuck's, I saw a tall, athletic, white-haired man talking energetically on his cell phone. I walked into the café, thinking it was a shame that man wasn't Antonio. But it was Antonio. His eyes, graceful movement, smooth skin, and clean features improved on closer inspection.

As we stood in line for our caffè lattes he shifted his weight from one foot to another, looking at me like a dog waiting for instructions. This fellow was hard to figure out—one minute imperious, the next minute nervous and unsure. He elbowed me aside firmly but politely when I reached into my purse to pay for my coffee.

The conversation rolled along well, but I had to get back to work. I was disappointed when he failed to make a follow-up date. He was by far the most handsome man I had ever even flirted with, and he bristled with energy.

I never saw Antonio again, and would never know why he acted the way he did. Little by little I was letting things happen without trying to control or understand them, but there was always a brief, sharp disappointment at parting.

Samuel also contacted me through Match.com, and we e-mailed back and forth a few times. He said he was a professor of statistics, specializing in agriculture. He traveled to conferences in Africa, Asia, and South America, and said he would take me with him. I took this invitation to be the ebullient fantasy phase of e-mail flirtation, but couldn't help but fantasize. I would never travel to Africa, Asia, or South America by myself.

After a few preliminary e-mails he wrote:

I do search for you, but I do so in the context of an open marriage.

What is an open marriage? Is it "See ya later honey, I've got a date," or do you all join in, or do you have periods like the French "cinq à sept"—certain hours or days when you each have time to yourself, no questions asked—or do you take separate vacations?

We arranged to meet at a coffee shop down the street from the Time/Life Building. I was almost there when my cell phone rang, and as I took the phone from my purse, I noticed a man walking on the other side of the street talking into his cell phone. I said, "I think I see you." We walked in parallel, on either side of the street, chatting for a few minutes without looking at each other, and only stopped our conversation when we reached out to shake hands. "Brave new world," I said.

"That was funny," he said, as he opened the door to usher me into the café.

He was older and less good-looking than his photograph, shorter than I was. By now that was standard.

Samuel was polite, warm, and paid for everything. The coffees and pastries were not expensive, but I was always conscious of the first-date precedent. The Internet was an egalitarian environment—women were as free to make the first move as men. It was altogether different from my days as a teenager, when I sat by the telephone waiting for a boy to ask me out (which happened only twice in high school). The boy always paid for everything. The men I was meeting had been raised in more or less the same social atmosphere, and I wondered how much of this childhood inequality of male and female could be erased. Intellectually, we would all *say* we were for the equality of women, but old habits die hard. I wasn't sure how to behave, and maybe these men weren't either. It was contradictory that a woman who could do the personal and professional things necessary to run a household and have a career should not be expected to pay for her own coffee, but it was more complicated than that. For the moment, if a man offered to pay, I accepted.

Samuel and I settled in and I talked too much about my job, my kids, my travels—every subject except the purpose of our meeting.

"Have you got any questions for me?" he asked abruptly.

"What's an open marriage?"

He jerked his head backwards as if I had struck him, then said, "It's a 'don't ask, don't tell' situation." He talked as if he were living like a teenager in his home, going out on dates, grateful that his mother—or in this case, his wife—didn't ask where he was last night. Abruptly, he said, "I'm sorry, I've got to get to an appointment. Please, finish your coffee, don't rush."

This felt like a brush-off, so his embroidered embrace—a warm kiss on the lips, further kisses to my neck, his hands running along my rib cage and back—confused me. "You're lovely," he said, kissing me once more before he left. I watched him through the plate glass windows as he walked quickly away.

I sensed him squirming to accommodate the Wife icon lodged in the matrix of his soul as he attempted to fulfill his own needs.

Two days later he wrote me a Zen saying, "even monkeys fall out of trees," and said he was like the money sitting on the ground trying to figure out how to climb back into the protective branches.

Married men have learned about that fine, strong cord beginning in the sex organs and running to the rest of the body and mind. When the cord reaches out like the tendril of a plant and wraps itself around another person, there is a connection that sucks in life as a plant devours sunlight. I felt that Samuel had been trying to wind that cord around me, make me the foundation for his own parasitic flowering, and I was grateful when he withdrew it, though a bit disappointed that I wouldn't be traveling to Asia, Africa, and South America.

The married men embraced their life-defining roles as husband and father, provider and protector—of their wives, not of me. Even if I had continued into a relationship with Antonio, Samuel, or even Malcolm, I would have existed in a secret place known only to the two of us. The prospect did not bother me. My life was unencumbered, simple, clear. I wanted to keep it that way. Let somebody else make their breakfasts, wash their underwear, be nice to their bosses.

I could find married men, but they didn't run deep. The ones I was meeting on the Internet badly needed a friend to talk to much more than they needed a female body to have sex with. A wise friend once said, "I think affairs are more about conversation than sex." Because their discontent and loneliness had to be hidden from their families and friends, these men had bottled up stores of feeling. I was ready to listen, but aware that The Wife is mistress of a man's deepest waters.

E-mails from married men cascaded like an avalanche of circus acts. In the end, I was sure of one thing: Partners who provide no touch bring the dry isolation of old age into youthful lives, sending their mates into one-handed telephone conversations with total strangers. Sex is the magma of life, and it erupts to the surface scalding and dangerous. If not allowed to flow freely, it will break through the fault lines of even the most earnest intention and discipline. The married men who contacted me showed how frequently the fault lines let the magma through. It had broken through in me, too.

· 24 ·

A Step Backward

After a while, I had had my fill of married men and stopped answering most of their e-mails. I had fun writing to Pete, though. He was a sixty-eight-year-old man who lived in New York with his wife and ten-year-old son. To this day, I don't even know his last name. He used to be a professional journalist but left to do something else, and was now taking care of his growing son. He was protective of his privacy, since he didn't want to harm his wife, who had put up with his womanizing for years. He expressed it this way:

After 22 years of fucking, she is the only woman I was ever happy finding in my bed the next morning.

We both loved writing, and frequent e-mails came naturally. Soon the printouts of my e-mails with Pete were a couple of inches high.

I told him of my confusion about married men, and he reminded me from the inside what marriage was like. Of sex with his wife he wrote, *Our intimacies are as rationed and ephemeral as a picnic in Fallujah.* He was sure that I was probably having better sex now than I would if I were married.

Soon, Pete knew a great deal about me and I knew a great deal about him, except his name and what he looked and felt like.

We wandered frequently onto tangents in our e-mails; for example, I told Pete about a man who said he had lost his virginity at seventeen when he visited a neighboring farm. The farm's owner, a woman twenty years older than he, was watching a stallion service her mare, and afterwards pushed my friend into a stall and pulled his pants down. He ejaculated before he could reach the Promised Land, but figured it out for the next time, and they had an off-and-on affair for forty years. He said that the last time he had sex with her she was seventy-seven and partially blind.

I elaborated in a tangent, which might have uncovered my sexual quirk. Pete was the first man I revealed this to:

I don't like watching nature programs on PBS because they show the tigers or the elephants or the horses humping away, and it turns me on. Even the little rabbits and mice turn me on. Insects and fish disgust me. Being fucked by a horse would not be fun in real life, but is occasionally nourishing in fantasy. There's something so urgent about it. The stallion circles the mare, the mare grazes and moves her behind out of reach, then the stallion nuzzles her and whispers in her ear, and she blushes and moves away again. He tries to contain himself, taking it out on the other stallions, then, finally, using his gentle insistence, convinces her and feels wild release.

Pete responded that an Italian psychoanalyst had the flanks

of a proud, prancing mare, but he had never found the opportunity to mount her from behind. When it came to sex, I couldn't stump him. He'd had one of everything.

Pete got bored washing the kitchen floor and doing the shopping, and I gave him pep talks, told him stories, and amused him. He reaffirmed my attractiveness in poetic e-mails, saying: There is something of the intrinsic Circe in you. There is nothing more attractive than a woman who unguardedly allows herself the freedom to express what she really is.

How sweet.

He claimed to have had sex with over 2,000 women. I called him a liar, but he insisted. He had lived in San Francisco during the Flower Child days, served in the Navy, worked in Denmark—all places reputed to be rich in willing women. After hearing some of his stories I gave him the benefit of the doubt. Statistically speaking, if a guy put his mind to it, he probably could get a couple of thousand women into his bed over a period of fifty years. That's forty a year. If he were married and reasonably faithful for half of the years, that might be 80 a year: one every 4.56 days. His secret was that he wasn't picky about his women. *What's more, most of the outstanding beauties, and there were a few, could have learned a thing or two from the bow wows.*

He was the person I wrote to from a meditation retreat:

Hi Pete: Today was the day for walking meditation. In a walking meditation you pay close attention to everything you come across. I looked at, and listened to, the dried fallen leaves under my feet, and imagined they were the souls of ancestors—entities which had done their job in life, fallen in death, robbed of their souls and spirits, and now lay at our feet for us to notice, some clumped together, others lying alone. I felt like my feet were crackling through my mother and my father, my grandmother. Of course the leaves disintegrate and disappear, as do our memories of our ancestors. The most recent ones are around for a while, in dessicated form, to remind us of their lives. While walking back and forth on my chosen meditation circuit on this beautiful farm, I would stop every once in a while and saw a different set of trees, a different vista, each time, and thought how much like life that is. What you remember as your environment is no longer your environment when you revisit it. There are new trees, maybe a silver horse, as appeared almost suddenly when I looked up. You walk the circuit of your life, and every time you stop to take stock, the view is different.

He wrote the next day, deeply shaken. His wife had walked past him unexpectedly at 2 a.m. while he was answering my e-mail. She had been barefoot, so he hadn't heard her approach. He'd realized how hurt she would be if she found out that he was having an intimate correspondence with another woman. We were communicating at a level where he never met his wife, at least not these days.

What was my role in protecting his wife from hurt, I wondered? I had taken no vow. I was not the morality police.

He stayed quiet for a couple of weeks, then reappeared with a philosophical e-mail about the unlikelihood that anyone would find everything they needed in one person, no matter what the arrangement. *You just do your best, and the rest is compromise. And small business management. And the (only real) sacred business of successfully raising children.*

A mature marriage like Pete's, a tree with knots in it, is a lifetime achievement that I was too old to hope for, but if another kind of "arrangement" appeared, it would be worth trying, and I would do my damndest to make it last.

· 25 ·

Turning to God

During my adult lifetime the unthinkable had happened . . . often. JFK and his brother Bobby were killed, then Lee Harvey Oswald. Martin Luther King, Malcolm X. Pan American Airlines went out of business. The Wall went up in Berlin. The Wall came down in Berlin. The Soviet Union fell. Vietnam happened. Watergate happened. 9/11 happened. Chernobyl happened. Even Nagasaki and Hiroshima happened during my lifetime, though I was too young to remember it.

Democracy has been gerrymandered and profiteered into a cartoon of itself; capitalism has become an oligarchy of the already-rich; Christianity has become a conspiracy of shouting, fanatical bullies; Islam has exploded into vicious medieval caricature; and marriage is a vestige of historical and biological circumstances which no longer exist. Couples are stuffed for ever-longer lives into a box fit only for Houdini. It won't be

me, but I hope someone else will come up with a new vision
for the world that will seem obvious when it appears, like
Gandhi's non-violence, like the Laws of Gravity.

Life had a slippery, uncertain feel.

The men I had interacted with were becoming blurred. A
man would refer to my profile and I couldn't remember what I
had written. Which man had a puppy? What was the name of
that man's daughter? Since first signing up for Classical Music
Lovers Exchange, I had e-mailed, talked on the phone, gone
out with, had sex with, and dated men ranging from a twenty-
nine-year-old television news producer to men in their sixties.
There were accountants, lawyers, a civil engineer, policemen,
doctors, writers, an inventor, a Louisiana farmer, an
astrophysicist, an oil rig engineer, entrepreneurs, a real estate
executive, a banker, several professors, a paralegal, salesmen,
unemployed guys, a journalist, a magazine editor, a computer
scientist, a stay-at-home dad, an architect, a private detective, a
goldsmith, a mortgage broker, a fireman, a chemist, a
psychoanalyst, a baseball umpire, and more. They were
married, divorced, separated, single, widowed. They lived
from Scotland and Germany to Hawaii. I watched what these
men did, what they promised, what they withheld, what they
wanted, how they saw themselves, what they thought of me.
All I was left with were questions about what was "right," what
was "normal," and what was expected.

What was my duty to the wives of the married men who
contacted me on the Internet? What was the "normal" sexual
appetite for sixty-year-old women? The expectations I had
been raised with were not how it was. What was the real
difference between men and women? I had raised my children
mostly by myself, was capable of doing almost everything a
man could do, and men seemed grateful to forego their
aggressor roles and be seduced. In what cache lay their egos?
And mine? Were we more precisely defined as "human" than

by our genders? Could women ask men out and pay for dinner without losing their femininity? Was marriage still the Holy Grail? Could younger men date older women? Was it okay for a sixty-year-old woman to have a baby? Married men (and presumably married women) went out with other people all the time, but there didn't seem to be any rules except "don't do it," which was regularly ignored. What moral rights did the Other Woman have? How much of the truth should children know? Should my children know what I was up to? Which moral judgments were worth holding on to and which were worthless?

It would be anarchic to have each individual making it up as she was going along (as I was), so there should be some ethical clearing house. I'd start with the church.

My Unitarian-Universalist minister put me in touch with his Catholic counterpart in Montclair, a blue-eyed, white-haired, middle-aged priest with a slight paunch. He stressed that his approach would be "pastoral, not theological." I didn't know what that meant, but okay.

I didn't regale him with tales of Ken, Howard, Frank, Antonio, Samuel, Hank, Michael, and all the others, but rather stuck to the question that bothered me the most at that time. "A lot of married men contact me through dating sites, and I'm not sure what to do with them. If I like them, should I go out with them? I'm not married; I didn't take a vow. What responsibility do I have to police somebody else's vows? Maybe his wife is ill, or doesn't have sex with him. Or maybe she is abusive or lives somewhere else—I don't know. Even if I could check on the man's veracity, it's not my business to judge other peoples' decisions."

The priest was ready for me. "Marriage is not a private arrangement, it is a public act. To be married in the Catholic Church you need a priest and two witnesses. The priest confirms the sacrament that the couple confer on each other.

The rules are not determined by the couple, but they must rely on each other to live up to them. The rest of us have a responsibility to help them live by their commitments. There is an obligation to respect the sacrament. It has to do with intention."

What pap! Who determined the "rules"? What were "their commitments"? How could I help someone else to "live by a commitment"? Did my listening to the grief of a husband who felt he was losing his manhood undermine his commitment, or did it help him redefine it, and perhaps live up to it better? What if, over a period of fifty or more years, a person's "intention" changed?

I wanted to get down to earth with this subject, without offending the good father. "These men write to me of things they say they can't talk to their wives about. Over a period of years, couples find that there are certain things they will never agree on, some of them very important. If the wives ever saw the correspondence between us, which touches on all the sensitive points between them, they might be devastated. Does this mean that I, or he, shouldn't have the correspondence?"

"If the wife discovers his e-mails, he just has to tell her that this is a friendship, not an affair, and hope she understands. He will have to take his stand on the truth. But you have to stay alert and note when signs emerge that things are changing."

"What does a man do if his wife won't have sex with him, or vice versa for that matter?"

"Then he won't have sex."

"But so few people can do that!"

"Celibacy has its virtues." He twinkled a smile.

"Oh, I know that well," I twinkled back.

The priest was enjoying our parrying, and not fazed by my questions. "What choice do they have? It's difficult, but that's what they have to do."

His pat answers led me to believe that this was not the first time he had had a similar conversation. I kept probing. "It seems as if marriage is too much for some people to sustain."

"The Church has become more nuanced in its assessment of marriage. It realizes that, psychologically, there are some people who are incapable of making a lifetime commitment, have a psychological incapacity to stick to something like that."

He said that it was still his "responsibility to represent the ideal." The goal of Christian marriage should be "sexual, not genital, energy"—which sounded as dense and incomprehensible as the religion I had been raised in, Christian Science. What, exactly, did that mean?

After what I had seen on the Internet, I thought he was spinning tales when he told me how blissfully happy and fulfilled some celibate people were. Maybe some people are asexual, but asexual people don't show up on the Internet. I consider them lucky in some ways. They can devote all of their energies to other matters. The Dalai Lama says that he has never needed sex.

Many Catholic priests and I had learned that deciding or vowing to be celibate is not enough. Some people may be able to resist the first tsunami of desire, but sooner or later all but the most resolute, or those lucky few who can turn it on and off, will drown in it. To the Montclair priest, sex was only supposed to exist within the sacrament of marriage, and therefore sex was divine—but both sex and marriage seemed purely human to me.

The priest regaled me about the prickly dilemmas his parishioners had experienced when they reached outside their marriages for sex. He said the Catholic Church had become "more sophisticated" regarding peoples' sexual anomalies and idiosyncrasies. "Sophistication" seemed to explain his statement at the beginning of our conversation that we would be having a "pastoral," not a "theological," discussion. This meant that he gave different advice from the pulpit than he gave in private conferences.

The theological goal and pastoral reality clashed, and this was the Catholic version of normal. But the grisly gulf between one and the other was seismically disturbing to me. So many people had been crushed between these millstones.

A flood of questions came to mind: "What about adopted children?" "If I get married, at my age, would that marriage be less valid, and less valuable, since I will not procreate?" "Is the marriage of an infertile couple similarly less valid and valuable?" "What if a couple decides they don't want children? Is that a sin?" "How many miscarriages, stillbirths, or other childbirth tragedies does the Church require a couple to go through before deciding not to try any more?" I imagined the answers given would feature the same theological sleight of hand, so I kept them to myself.

My own Unitarian-Universalist minister said that couples should make their own agreements and stick to them. We concurred that forging a unique agreement was a much harder assignment than accepting a pre-packaged one, but once agreed upon, it would be easier to uphold. If circumstances changed, the agreement could be changed to conform.

I asked him, "Are there people in our congregation who have what they call open marriages?"

"Oh yes. I don't, though. It would be too much trouble."

There didn't seem to be much more to say. People did what they needed to do, and as long as the integrity of the couple's vows to each other was not violated and people were treated respectfully, this church would support them. I didn't see anything wrong with this approach.

The Unitarian-Universalist minister thought the public marriage ceremony was incidental, while the Catholic priest thought marriage was a public, not a private, act. There was another glaring difference: in the Catholic Church's eyes, marriage was for procreation, while Unitarian-Universalists determined its purpose for themselves.

Obviously, guaranteeing that procreation was not polluted with random sperm would necessarily mean that couples would have to be faithful to one another. That system was desirable, but had also guaranteed that European royal families would be cursed with hemophilia as the contaminated bloodlines were reinforced.

I might also have gone to the Lutheran minister, and the Mormon bishop, and the Evangelical pastor, but I had my answer. In my relationships, fidelity would be defined as keeping to a mutually agreed arrangement. The initial terms I would require were still not clear, and might differ from my partner's, but I took more seriously the prospect of discussing and hewing to whatever I and some future partner agreed to. I would also be leery of taking up with Catholics and others whose religion required double think.

My rules regarding married men were that if a younger man who had been married only a few years was seeking an affair, I dismissed him out of hand because he had not yet shown a good faith effort to make his marriage successful. But I would take older married men one by one. Some men said their wives were physically or mentally ill. Some were confessed habitual philanderers, like Pete, whose wife had long ago adjusted to him flirting with women in the elevator. Some, like Malcolm, were seeking a cybersex supplement. Some were sincerely trying to fill out their lives with a meaningful relationship. Some, like Samuel, claimed open marriages. Many of them had done their duty raising children and keeping the family together, and now that the kids were gone they were looking elsewhere for someone to talk to.

Some felt trapped: one man wrote, *I am never again going to have a sympathetic female companion, never going to have the sex that I am still capable of having, never again going to feel like a man.* He wasn't alone in his concern over the loss of swaggering control over erections. It was now or never.

There were times during my own two marriages when returning home was like returning to prison. I had done everything I could think of to keep both marriages alive, but they were not salvageable. The problems in my marriages were not sexual, and could not have been healed through sex with another man, and at the time I was committed to monogamy. There were no simple feelings involved, and no easy rules. I understood what these married men were feeling.

Just how pitiful are the numbers on successful marriages? If fifty percent of marriages end in divorce, and among the surviving fifty percent a certain percentage of spouses engages in extramarital affairs or is living a life of celibate fortitude, what are the odds of establishing a "happy" marriage? How can we support our social archetypes and expectations on such a slender outcome? Do we care about the welfare of those who are living lives of celibate fortitude, or only about the bad behavior of those having affairs? Is the institution of marriage worth the sacrifice of oneself?

I would continue to look for my own arrangement.

· 26 ·

No Harmony

On May 2004, I went to a new doctor who asked me if I was sexually active, and I admitted to sex with three different men in the past eight months. Unsurprised (at least outwardly), he told me that I should be sure to ask my gynecologist to check for venereal disease. Besides the occasional visit from Frank, however, I wasn't having sex with anybody anymore. Ken was with Elaine, Howard was with his mother, and none of the other flirtations had become relationships.

I was taking one situation at a time, but had no idea where my project was headed. The dating conventions I had grown up in seemed ridiculous. Stage one was "going steady," when a girl wore a boy's ring around her neck; stage two was getting pinned, when she wore his fraternity pin on her blouse; stages three and four were the engagement ring and the wedding band. There were no further stages.

In this new world, I had achieved my first goal: finding a man or men to have sex with. I was confident that I could easily find another Ken or Howard. It was time to move the bar higher. My next goal was establishing a reliable, supportive relationship of some sort. My own efforts had not worked out, so I paid for eHarmony to do the work for me. I anticipated that I wouldn't learn as much, but using their system would save me time.

I took their exhaustive personality evaluation, filled out their forms, and sat back waiting for my lollipop. While I was waiting, eHarmony flogged its Christian books, not answering my e-mail asking why they were proselytizing on a dating site. Someone later told me that it was a Christian organization; their goal was to promote marriage between Christians. I had to laugh, I really did. I did not fit their customer profile at all, because I was not going to procreate—the goal of "Christian" marriage. Why waste their efforts on an old lady when they could snare a young one who could give birth to more Christians?

Having taken my money, they still had to do their job. They informed me that I was so "unusual" that I might have to wait six weeks before receiving a match. What was unusual about me? Today's world is full of women my age who hope to add romance back into their lives. I felt dismissed and freaky.

About a month later, two weeks earlier than expected, I received a match. The gentleman was an African-American professor of accounting at a university on Long Island. I wrote a short get-to-know-you note in the space eHarmony provided. They did not reveal Mr. Professor's name or e-mail to facilitate direct communication. Two weeks later I received a notification that Mr. Professor was "too busy to pursue a relationship at this time." That was a soft landing for a hard dismissal. Was it because I was white? Too old? Wrong religion? Too far away? It was creepy having a third party do the romantic negotiation, and I didn't like it.

A few weeks later they sent me a match with an eighty-three-year-old retiree, and then a seventy-five-year-old retiree. I would be hypocritical if I scrubbed these men because they were much older than I was. If a man twenty-five years my junior could go out with me, as Ken had, shouldn't I be ready to date a man twenty-three years my senior? We exchanged e-mails.

The eighty-three-year-old had been born in the 1920s. He would have romanced his sweetheart to "I'll See You Again" and "Chattanooga Choo Choo," maybe even Al Jolson. He might have served in the Second World War, as did my father. He could have been raising his own children when television appeared. I, too, remember "Chattanooga Choo Choo" playing on my breadbox-sized radio when I was a child, and remember when a neighbor got the first television on the block and I got to see *Howdy Doody*, but my sensibilities were formed in the '60s and '70s by Bob Dylan, Pete Seeger, Joan Baez, Elvis Presley, and The Beatles.

Also, younger men were less likely to have been raised with poisonous ideas about women who liked sex. My young sex buddies relished my libido.

The eHarmony older men were constrained by an excess of good manners. They politely answered questions about themselves, their children, and their former marriages by giving me facts and figures. They initiated conversations by mentioning the books they had read and the plays they had seen, but their spirits were veiled. It would be unbearable to retreat within myself to a point where I could be compatible and comfortable with these men. These were the kinds of people I had run away from when I was a young woman.

There are many women who would find their gentle-manly approach a breath of fresh air in the raunchy world of today, but I wrote to eHarmony asking to revise my age parameters. They answered that it would be best if I left the choosing of my mate up to them.

I resigned.

· 27 ·

And Now, About Me

I was a sculptor chipping away at the rock to find the statue within, surprised at what I found. My natural self would have been a good courtesan in olden days. I would have refused to submit to a bouncing, eager boy whose intellect and strength might have been a shadow of mine. My friends would have vowed to obey these eager boys, their bellies would have swelled into babies, and their spirits would have turned inward, hearthward.

The king would have loved my full breasts, my long legs and neck, my smile, ready laughter, teasing wit, and open, affectionate nature. The look in other men's eyes as I passed by would raise his cock. He would have loved my dancing, my singing, my savory dinners. I would have been one of the few people who didn't flatter (unless the truth itself was flattery).

He would have told me his secrets—the loss of a friend, festering anger, and how, on a visit to Spain, the Duchess had tied him to a bedpost using rough nautical rope and flayed him with a satin ribbon, suddenly reaching for her riding crop when satin was no longer sufficient.

He would have cried at getting older, and confessed his desire for the dimpled chambermaid.

Our intimate secrets would have bound us tightly enough to traverse my aging. When he looked at my still-graceful body, he would have loved me. His secrets and his love would have aged like wine, he more knowing, more wistful. I would have found security, and he would have found comfort.

Who am I kidding? I had gone for the hearth and the swollen belly, and felt very fortunate to live in modern times, when a woman could divorce and stand alone if she needed to.

Life as a modern-day courtesan was interesting, but the limbo of this life was causing me pain and worry. I am sure Madame de Pompadour felt the same. I found myself wanting to occupy a place in a good man's life. I wanted to be the first person he shared an opinion with, someone he craved if we were apart.

It sounded banal—I wanted someone to love me.

· 28 ·

Ernest: The Halcyon Days

had sufficient new experience now to think back on the gnarly mess of my two failed marriages without the clutch of repugnance or shame in my gut. It was important to think about these things as I tried to define the arrangement I was looking for now.

It was particularly important to come to terms with my marriage to Ernest. Our divorce had involved abuse, poverty, and despair, and I had dumped the whole mess into a personal black hole so hatred and shame would not infect the rest of my life. I would probably never stray near outright abuse again, but there were miles of uncharted territory between endgame abuse and a first date. What I feared most was delusion—doing something I thought was different but was in fact a repetition of the same old patterns.

I met Ernest in Athens, Greece in 1968, when I was twenty-six years old and he was thirty-seven. I was teaching

English at the Hellenic-American Union on steep Massalias Street, near the university. After siesta, I left my one-room apartment on Odos Deinodratous, picked up a cheese pie, and ate it walking past sluggish, awakening janitors seated in front of their apartment houses. Housewives and maids passed me clutching their shopping bags. Butchers sleepily rang up their steel protective gates.

After classes, we teachers would eat together in the cheap, old-fashioned *tavernas* with rough-hewn tables, flagstone or dirt floors, and waiters who took orders orally, even with fifteen people at the table.

When I brought my guitar, we'd sing. Passing Greeks knew "Leavin' on a Jet Plane" or "The House of the Rising Sun" or some other popular song, and would either stop to listen or join in.

Life was easy, but it was time to think about settling down. Greeks had their ways and their clans, and I would forever be a foreigner in Athens, no matter how well I spoke the language. My friends were expatriates from America, Australia, Britain, Denmark. They came and went, giving a tenuous, impermanent feel to all of my relationships. I didn't want to go home to New Jersey or New York. I was still thinking every day about a man I had cared for very much who had left me to go back to his wife. I had been lonely in New York; in Athens, I was lonely in a different way.

Slanting upwards outside the window of my apartment was the stairway leading up Mt. Lycavittos, and passersby could hear me singing and playing the guitar. On his way up the steps one evening, an Australian journalist named Ernest was intrigued by the singing. We met at an evening party a few days later, and he realized I was the singer. He urged me to sing again, and afterwards a few of us walked to a family restaurant perched on the shoulder of Mt. Lycavittos. He walked me home, and we talked and made love until dawn.

He wasn't the sort of person I had in mind as a boyfriend: He was four inches shorter than me, stocky and bearded, with haunting blue-grey eyes. His manner was passionate, pugnacious, bright, and vulnerable. He said he was working on a book about Greece and supported himself giving sporadic private English lessons.

According to him, then and forever after, even in the worst of our times, it was love at first sound. His aggressive certainty about everything, including me, relieved me of the responsibility of figuring out what I wanted to do. He moved in with me a month after we met, and we were together almost every day for the next fourteen years, seven of them in Greece and seven in Montclair, New Jersey.

WHEN WE FIRST MET, Ernest and I were kindred spirits. We flung aside convention and did what we saw in front of us. We had each chosen to flee our culture, our religion, and our family. They all said "no" too much.

I should have left Ernest on that evening in Athens when, drunk with ouzo, he barked at me, "Bring me a glass of water!" "Make the bed." "Clean up the kitchen." He was muscular and had a black belt in jujitsu. Opposing him might have meant injury to me, so I quietly did as I was told, but I was seething. Over breakfast the next day, I said I didn't want to see him again, but he claimed not to remember the night before. He attributed his abusiveness to the ouzo and swore never to drink ouzo again.

Our halcyon days followed. As American and Australian citizens, we were free of the rules that governed the Greeks around us. We didn't even have to pay taxes. We were intrepid, curious, free. My circle of expat friends widened from my fellow teachers to Ernest's journalist friends to the head of chancery of the British Embassy, with whom I played piano duets, his wife impatiently announcing again and again that dinner was ready as we failed again and again to tear ourselves away from the piano. Our Greek acquaintances were policemen, generals, artists, and students whom Ernest had met while researching his book. Classes took only a portion of every day, and I didn't work for thirteen weeks between semesters in the summertime, so our schedule was open and flexible.

Friends vacated a spacious apartment in the Metz section of Athens, next to the Stadium at the foot of the Royal Gardens, and we moved there. There were three large, high-ceilinged rooms, a spacious kitchen, and a deep terrace. A corner of the Acropolis was visible from our window. I hung the laundry on a clothesline strung on the fire escape outside our kitchen door, and in summer it blew dry in minutes.

The rent was a thousand drachmas, about $30, a month. My salary was $100 a month. Every Tuesday night we played badminton with a rowdy crowd of Australians and Britons. This was not the schoolgirls' game I had grown up with but a fast-moving scramble to hit a birdie that might travel 120 miles an hour. After our games, the Badminton Club caroused at our favorite *taverna*. Most main dishes in Greece were overcooked and pedestrian, but the appetizers, called *mezedes*, were marvelous: fried *kalamarakia*; eggplant puffs filled with feta cheese; *xoriatiki salata* with fresh tomatoes, zingy olives, crunchy green peppers, fragrant olive oil, and tart feta cheese; thin slices of battered fried zucchini; *papoutsakia*, shoe-shaped pastries filled with meat or cheese; *tzatziki*, yoghurt with garlic, cucumber, and dill; *taramosalata*, a smooth spread made from fish eggs; freshly fried potatoes; and my favorite, *pastitsio*, the Greek version of macaroni and cheese, with a béchamel sauce over the macaroni, browned on top. There was crunchy bread, too, and thick glass carafes of local *retsina* wine.

We spent one Greek Easter in a village perched on a steep hillside in Epirus and watched the midnight procession, which strung a necklace of flickering candlelight along a mountain path winding up to the church. The next day smelled of roasting lamb and oregano. Such sights, tastes, and smells surge in my memory even today.

One summer, we visited the tiny island of Kos, just off the Turkish coast. The doors of our hotel room opened onto the wine-dark sighing sea, lulling us to sleep. The next day we took the ferry across to Bodrun, Turkey and under the canopy of a beach restaurant I had the best mashed potatoes of my life, slightly runny, and smooth. The Turkish women on the beach didn't swim, but rather walked far out in the shallow waters, splashing water on themselves. As they inched farther and farther out, their pantaloons ballooned. The rotund older women's huge black balloons were surrounded by the smaller satellite balloons of the young girls attending them.

On another trip we took a country walk in the Peloponnesus and came across a smiling farmer dressed in baggy black woolen pants and a worn blue cotton shirt. Suspenders held up his baggy pants. He carried a hoe over his shoulder, like a Russian peasant in *War and Peace*, only his setting was olive groves and fields of artichokes instead of wheat.

The farmer gestured excitedly as he told how German troops had come over that hill right over there into his town during the Second World War. He said they weren't so afraid of the German troops, but they were terrified of the Communists during the Civil War that came later. During the twin wars they continued harvesting their olives, artichokes, and tomatoes, milking their goats, making their feta cheese, and plucking fish from the sea.

To us, a conversation with a farmer was more valuable than a visit to Agamemnon's palace, though we did that too.

· 29 ·

Ernest: The River of Bile

Ernest had both repugnance and fascination regarding Greece. He thought their systems were dysfunctional and stupid, and he never learned even basic Greek, but he was fascinated by their predictability; the whole country ran in phases. The title of the book he was writing was *The Cycle* because the same events kept repeating themselves in Greek history with no effort to break the pattern. One day they were all pro-American, the next day they were all anti-American, or anti-Germany, or pro-the King. Rumors and current events aroused the Greek love of emotional outburst unsupported by intellectual investment. Ernest confronted authority often and passionately, and perhaps he wanted to stay in Athens because it felt safe to explode occasionally there. And the weather reminded him of his hometown, Brisbane, Australia.

Ernest's press credentials gave him access to the no man's

land between police lines and protesters against the dictator, Papadopoulos, and he pulled me in with him. There was battlefield camaraderie between the two factions, with the students chanting in the rhythmic Middle-Eastern way—daDAH, daDAH, daDAH-daDAH-daDAH—and the poker-faced police, who stood silent. The antagonists never surged toward each other, which would have squeezed us at the heart of the fray. I wasn't frightened, but on a later evening I would have reason to be.

In November 1973, students at the university again exploded in revolt against Papadopoulos. Ernest's journalistic instincts went into gear, and we installed ourselves in a café on Omonia Square, waiting for something to happen. Army trucks appeared, barreling round and round the fountain. I caught a foul smell, and Ernest muttered, "Tear gas." He poured water on our thick bar napkins, handed me one, and we put them over our noses and mouths and calmly walked away from the square, trying not to draw the attention of the soldiers in the trucks. He had covered violent protests in Paris and a war in Algeria, and knew some of the tricks of salvation. The cardinal rule was not to act guilty.

We could see bonfires burning in the spoke-like avenues leading onto the square, protesters silhouetted against the vaulting flames. We took the back way home along one of the dirt roads winding under the Acropolis. We could barely see where we were going, and tripped over stones and branches. Suddenly, a harsh voice commanded, "Left, right, left, right" in Greek, and the unison tramp of booted feet grew louder and louder. We had a quick, whispered discussion. If we hid among the trees and the soldiers spied us, they might take us for fleeing protesters. If we met them directly on the road they might think the same, but our chances would be better if we acted like innocent tourists, so we kept walking. The soldiers tramped past ten yards below us on a parallel road, and didn't see us at all, but it was a while before my heart stopped thumping.

Ernest recorded our interviews and his descriptions and commentary on a tape recorder. After every adventure there were tapes to transcribe. Transcribing a single conversation, which required rewinding and close listening, might take hours. I am a freakily fast typist, and offered to support his work by transcribing his tapes. After seven years of my diligent labor, he had compiled a knee-high pile of papers, but they sat there unused. He did not make any effort to show his work to agents or publishers. I became resentful. I was teaching and transcribing, and he was bringing in less and less money. That was the second time that I should have left him.

But he told me again and again how much he loved me. By submitting to his plan for life, I had lost some of my own initiative, and our lives were entwined financially and personally. I was also far from people who knew me well enough to counsel me. Something I had lacked in my childhood—constant support and companionship—became indispensable, but it would have been unavailable even if I had returned home. They were cool and reserved.

When I got pregnant in 1976 I insisted we return to Montclair, New Jersey, my hometown. I did not want my child born a Greek citizen. We married in Elkton, Maryland three weeks before our son was born, and two years later had a daughter. Gone were the raucous nights in *tavernas*, the long vacations, the café life, and the self-indulgence. It was then that the river running through him slowly turned to bile.

We opened a word processing service on Bloomfield Avenue in Montclair so I could have the children with me every day. Ernest puttered around, but never brought in so much as a month's rent.

Gradually, my friends and family recoiled from Ernest's confrontational behavior. His goal, possibly unconscious, of separating me from those who loved me was accomplished, even when we lived in the same town. I didn't have the energy to resist his will. I was supporting the family financially by working every day at our business, doing the cooking, shopping, laundry, and cleaning, and taking care of the kids. Like abusive spouses everywhere, he was keeping me too busy to object.

I had been having pain in my shoulders and neck, and it became worse and worse. I would go grey for one or two days a month, unable to get out of bed. My shoulders and neck would turn to cement. It was hard to open my eyes because the glare of sunlight heightened the pain all over. When this happened, Ernest would snort in derision and say, "Just get up and take a warm bath." It was years before I got a diagnosis: fibromyalgia.

It was a long time before I even thought of divorce. That would separate the family and nullify solemn vows. Ernest was spiraling downward, though, and I had to do something. I told my mother I was thinking of leaving Ernest. She said, "Thank God!"

I was stunned.

My mother did her thinking alone, inscrutable, and until she was ready to speak it was useless to pry. Since she was so wound up about whatever it was by the time she spoke out, the ensuing conversations were freighted with emotion, and discussions became confrontations. My life was dotted with hurtful maternal explosions, the majority of which involved my admittedly ill-considered romantic life. In all things, romantic and otherwise, she used the Overwhelming Force Theory and made sure that after our discussion things were not the same. Now, for once, we coalesced, and she gave me money to see a lawyer, who terrified me by telling me all the awful things that could happen when I began divorce proceedings. Nothing could pulverize my resolve, though. I needed to be free, with my children.

An acquaintance invited me to coffee, where I met a round woman in her late fifties named Margaret Pawska. She got an earful about my pitiful situation, and then we discovered that both of us played the piano and were enthusiastic cooks. We could banter in French and had both been raised Christian Scientists. Our conversation reminded me that there was a safe, interesting world waiting for me when I could get free. I didn't want to be accused of kidnapping, so I waited for the court date to free me. After that, I had no plans. My mother offered me and the children three weeks of hospitality. Three weeks to settle the children in school, find child care, find a job —it was almost offensive, but without her, I would have had no hope at all of freedom.

The next day, Margaret telephoned me. "When you can, why don't you move in with me? I don't use the second floor anyway, so if you want to clear it out, you can stay there."

Instead of living on welfare, the children and I could live in Margaret's drafty, cavernous Victorian house on Orchard Street in Bloomfield. She also offered to watch the children after school.

When I could steal an hour away from our business, I brushed away the cobwebs in the four rooms on Margaret's second floor, vacuumed every nook and cranny, and shined up the windows.

As the court date approached I was nervous. Ernest could spin the tale of a talented, courageous war correspondent, world traveler, and devoted father. He could regale the judge about his friendship with our son's karate teacher and his constant attendance at our daughter's ballet class (while I was slaving away at our business).

Desperate though I was, I had only touched the hem of agony.

· 30 ·

Ernest: Vanquished

The Friday before the first court date, Ernest took the car and all the money from our joint bank account and kidnapped the children. Contemplating life without my children felt like death. Then one day I was stopped at a red light in Montclair—corner of Watchung and Valley—and a calm descended. If my children were taken from me, or if he spitefully killed them, I would live on. It was as simple as that. I would give my life for my children, but they would be left with no protector if I died. I needed to be victorious, and victory would come from my own strength.

He made increasingly outlandish daily telephone calls. My resolve turned to stone, and a fury developed that was well beyond words.

With the pressure of a Bench Warrant for his arrest, he brought them back after five days on the run, and the children and I moved to Margaret's house. My mother paid our modest r nt. She may have been an imperfect support, but when moments of collapse came, she stepped forth time and again.

One or two days a month I was bedridden with fibromyalgia headaches and incapacitating fatigue, and on those days Margaret took over. I sank into a warm bath, then I went to bed. With every moment of warmth and security, I became stronger.

We were an odd little family. Since Margaret was there to watch over the children after school, I could get a job. I was a weak reed, and Margaret was a steady hand with the children. They learned music, they ate good food, they had a kind person to come home to.

The judge denied Ernest visitation. In my mind, he had renounced every right as a parent. I would take care of myself, my son, and my daughter. Ernest threatened us again and again in the ensuing years, but he was vanquished.

Even the closest family and friends are prey to forces others can't see. I have scanned Ernest's life for the clues to his collapse into sociopathy and abuse, but can only make assumptions about what was washing around inside him. He had suffered shocks, indignities, and illnesses, but hadn't we all? He never, by the way, finished even a first draft of the book he had started before we met.

All along, I had been prisoner not to Ernest, but to a naïve fantasy of myself as the archetypal, sacrificial Muse, a modern-day Anna Dostoyevski.

I'd gleaned a lot from those desperate years, and now, as I reviewed my past, I promised not to stuff another destructive relationship into my basket of dreams. If I didn't find what I wanted, then life alone, even celibate, had its virtues. Either way I would be fine.

· 31 ·

Benjamin

I had begun writing books and essays myself, and doubted that I would give that up again in service of another person's writing career, but it's eerie how people will think they are choosing lovers who are different from the ones who deeply disappointed them, but are actually choosing people who will disappoint them in the same way. At sixty, I didn't have enough life left to sacrifice a decade or more on another fraudulent Prince Charming. Years of solitude and celibacy had refreshed my mind and loosened my spirit, and I now had to figure out my own life.

As usual, Pete expressed my situation succinctly: *Sex recharges you, but then what?*

The logy yellow heads of the daffodils in my garden knew spring was coming. A year and a half had passed since my first date with Stuart. I worked, and still swam thirty laps every evening. It had been good for me to step back and think things over before getting back into the game. I continued reading the dating sites, but the same faces popped up; I knew all of their gambits. The search was getting dull.

In May 2004, I learned about Craigslist, where there is no list of questions to answer, no guides or suggestions. A man wrote what he was thinking. Good writers coexisted with weird ones—one woman posted that she was stunned when a man paid $250 for her used tampon, which he put in his mouth. On Craigslist you posted your truth, whatever it was. Bruce and Samuel had lied about their age and weight on Match.com, and their pictures were a decade old. Maybe it was better to let people write what they wanted and manually weed out the weird ones.

I responded to a posting by a divorced professor, Benjamin. He suggested meeting at a café on the Upper West Side. He described himself as shorter than I and wrote cryptically, *I weigh more in winter than in summer.* He had brown hair, blue eyes, and was *considered handsome.*

On the appointed day I stood in front of the café. How do you stand while waiting for someone you've never met? Do you constantly look around? Do you try to rest a smile on your lips? Do you relax your face, running the risk that you look too serious or unfriendly? Do you read a book? I settled on an attitude of benign interest in the passing world.

One leftward glance caught a man in a blue blazer and blue jeans striding toward me, looking straight at me.

After we shook hands, he looked at me for a moment without speaking and I popped a smile on my face. He didn't seem to know what to do, but then said, "Where would you like to sit? Inside or outside?"

"Inside please. It's a little chilly. But let's sit near the window so we can watch the people going by."

"You got it." He opened the door for me.

I shucked my jacket and hung my purse on the back of my chair. He watched me analytically, as if he were thinking, "She looks okay. What do I want to do with this woman? Wait a while? Make a date for this weekend? Take her back to the apartment and give her dinner, kiss her a few times and sleep on it? Or do I want to fuck her brains out tonight?"

We got to know each other over a glass of wine. There was a white line along his gums where they met his teeth, and he didn't open his mouth much when he smiled, so I got the impression that he hadn't been to the dentist for years. I can't understand why a person would not go to the dentist, but he was not the first man I'd known who avoided dentists. Without asking him point-blank, "Why are your teeth such a mess?" I couldn't diagnose the problem. I would not want to kiss him very often.

As for his weight, he had said he was heavier in winter, and it was deep winter. A double chin was developing, but the muscles under his paunch suggested he really did play squash twice a week. He was pleasant, had an interesting career, seemed to love his family, and looked as if he were attracted to me. He had a pompous way of sitting, straight up, as if he feared being shouted at for slumping. He didn't flow fluidly; he bounced and jerked and jumped from place to place and from subject to subject.

He blurted out, "Shall we go back to my place and order in? I'm thinking Greek. There's a great Greek restaurant down the street and they deliver."

The call was sixty-forty. There were no rumblings of fabricated charm or underlying anger in Benjamin; he looked sincere and well intentioned. We had academic interests in common, and I liked the Upper West Side. It was worth a shot.

"Sounds delicious." I answered in the same tone of voice I would have used if he had asked me to go with him to the post office.

We turned right onto a street lined with townhouses and trees a couple of blocks from the café. Benjamin greeted the doorman, "How are you, Pablo?" "Very well, sir, how are you." We walked to the elevator and I repeated "Pablo Pablo Pablo" to myself so I would remember his name. I wondered how I measured up against the other women Benjamin must have brought home.

· 32 ·

Benjamin's Apartment

enjamin's apartment had a small foyer with a tapestry on the wall, and to the left a long, rectangular living room with four large windows facing the street. Matching Buddhas smiled on red lacquered tables at each end of the couch, and oriental prints hung on the walls. I guessed they were Japanese, but Benjamin said they were Korean. The wooden cabinet with oriental brass hardware contained the stereo system. His choice of Mozart's Clarinet Concerto was felicitous because my son had been a virtuoso clarinetist when he was a teenager and that piece always engaged my heart.

The bookcases along one wall were packed with books. Twin piles, one *The New York Times* and the other *The Wall Street Journal,* were stacked neatly on either side of his light brown leather easy chair. I sat on the couch and relaxed into green plush pillows.

We sorted out our preferences for dinner and he phoned in the order, then sat down next to me and put his feet on the wooden coffee table; I followed suit.

"So what do you think?" He surveyed the living room.

"You've done a really nice job decorating, and you must be a good housekeeper—or does someone do it for you?"

"No. No. I don't like people nosing around. I do it myself, and you're right, I like to keep it nice. I work here and I live here."

He pulled my head onto his shoulder and stroked my arms and back as he talked quietly. I reached my hand up to hold his hand. The affection was delicious.

"Do you like Mozart?"

"I especially like the clarinet concerto. My son used to play it."

"Aaah. My sons are more into sports."

"Which sports?"

"Baseball mostly."

"Do you play?"

"No, I play squash."

"Oh yeah. You said that in your profile. Sorry."

"Most of the things in my profile aren't true, but the thing about squash is." His self-deprecating humor made me more open to our continuing trade of affection. While such stroking might qualify as foreplay, it was not aggressive; it was quiet, reserved, sensual.

"I haven't been on a date in a year," he said.

"Really? Why?"

"I had a hard time getting over another woman. She sort of dropped me."

"You had been expecting more?"

"I thought I wanted to marry her."

"You thought?"

"I don't know, it's all very confusing to me. Very painful."

The conversation continued in a melancholy vein. He told about his grief from the recent loss of a sister, and as he spoke of her, he changed position again and again, trying to get comfortable in his own skin, tears poised in his eyes. Was this depression a deal-breaker? I thought not. Everyone is entitled to sadness over such loss.

"You're obviously still very upset about that too," I comforted him—I hoped.

"I guess we all have our crosses to bear. What about you?"

"Yikes. Two marriages, two divorces. Both of them were pretty challenging, but they were a while ago. I hadn't dated in twelve years, but since last fall I've gotten back into the swing of it."

"Oh. So we have a long time with no dates in common."

I laughed. "What a funny thing to have in common."

By the time the food arrived, I liked him more than I had in the café. He was forthright about his fragile emotional condition, and softly affectionate. He was obviously solvent, though his sanity remained in doubt. I had accompanied my second husband, Tom, on a devastating journey into manic depression, and would never want to go through that again, so I felt cautious.

Benjamin paid the delivery person, closed the door, then turned to me and said, "You stay right where you are. I'm a tyrant in my kitchen. It's so small."

"You don't seem like a tyrant," I teased.

"You know what I mean. It's easier to work in here by myself because it's so small. Besides, I want to take care of you," he said, peeping out at me briefly.

I curled up on the couch and closed my eyes. Someone else was taking care of dinner.

After dinner we watched part of a Mets game—the television was in the bedroom. Then, after mediocre sex, I slept next to a man for the first time in thirteen years. A presence next to me didn't protect me from djinns or dangers, but it shielded me from loneliness. When I moved my leg, he moved his. When I turned on my side, he patted me. During sex, he turned me away from him, which made me feel generic. Confronted only by a back, I could have been anybody.

· 33 ·

A Relationship Begins

At seven fifteen the next morning Benjamin's cell phone awakened us. He vaulted out of bed, picked up the phone, and walked out of the room, closing the door behind him. I could hear a whispered "Hi" as he walked down the passage to the living room.

"Here comes the deal-breaker," I thought to myself.

When he came back five minutes later, he said cheerily, "Let's find out what the weather's going to be today." He turned on TV1. "I'll make us breakfast. Take your time. I've put up a towel for you in the bathroom so you can take a shower if you like."

I barely knew this man, so it wasn't time for the third degree about the phone call. If it was anyone important, I would learn soon enough. I sang in the shower, got dressed, and went out to join him.

On the table lay a plate with two croissants (had he

thought ahead?), and two glasses of orange juice.

We read the paper for a while like an old married couple, and suddenly he gave me a hangdog look. "There's something I have to tell you about." He averted his eyes as he spoke. "There's another woman you should know about. I said 'know about,' not 'worry about.' She calls me every morning after her walk and every evening. I don't see her often, but we talk every day."

I tamped down my instinctive dismissal of our relationship. "Tell me about her."

"Her name is Lila. She has brain cancer and five years ago they said she had three years to live, but she's still working, still writing a poem every day. She's misshapen after several surgeries, but her hold on life is strong."

"That's amazing."

"She's an amazing person." He took down one of three deep boxes that sat side by side on the top bookshelf. This one was made of a heavy tan cardboard, with a nubbly texture and warm sheen to it. He reverently took the top off and revealed a foot-high stack of 8 ½ x 11 sheets of paper. "I print out her poems. She has created a little world where the creatures, the trees, and the humans are equally alive. Would you like to read one?"

"Sure."

He handed me a printout of an e-mail which began:

Dearest Benjamin: Here's the poem for this morning. I'm thinking of you.

The poem was something about birds in the spring. The "Dearest Benjamin" threw me. I pretended to read it and handed it back to him, "Lovely."

He carefully put the top back on the box and replaced it on its shelf. "She thinks of me as her lover, but we only had sex once or twice, years ago. We never even kiss now because she has to be careful of infection. She doesn't have any family except her sister, who suffers from multiple sclerosis, so I'm her health care advocate and advisor."

"This sounds like a deep relationship."

He took my hand and looked in my eyes. "I think it's only right that you should know about Lila before we go any further. I love her, and she loves me, but she is no impediment to my having another relationship."

"If we continued going out, would you tell her about me? Would I meet her?"

"I don't know. I don't even see her myself very often. Only Passover, her birthday, and whenever she has to go to the hospital. Sometimes at other times, but not often."

"How often does she go to the hospital?"

"She's got cancer, so . . ."

I ran my hand through my hair. "This is a little strange."

"It's entirely up to you, of course. I completely understand if this is unacceptable to you."

I searched for my true feelings. "I don't want to feel in competition with her. I'll have to think about it. This is unexpected."

"Of course."

We left the apartment, and he hailed a taxi and accompanied me to Penn Station. He walked me to the concourse and stroked my hand. "I had a wonderful time with you. You are a lovely, lovely person, and we should get together again soon. If you want to." He gathered me in and kissed my cheek. Strangers would have thought he was an ardent lover.

· 3 4 ·

A New York Girl

This was the most promising date so far. I was getting an MA in linguistics, and he was a professor of history. We both were about the same age, had two grown children, and had been divorced. Nobody gets to be sixty-one without a few scars and quirks. I was still very skittish about the mere idea of marriage, and he was still grieving his losses. Benjamin's sadness and anguish did send up a disturbing flag; on the other hand, being in that apartment and having someone to sleep next to had felt so good. Since I had no intention of giving up other men, it would be hypocritical to object that Benjamin was helping a beloved friend to her death, so I tended toward accepting the situation. If I was to be a free woman, I was obliged to allow him to be a free man.

The next few times we saw each other, he was in a much better mood, and we established a regular habit of spending

Tuesday and Friday nights together. We didn't correspond or
speak on the phone much between visits, but before I left each
time we would make a plan for our next night together. I loved
leaving work and boarding the uptown number 1 train. I was
"home" in half an hour instead of the hour and a half it took to
go back to Montclair. He pampered me, cooking and paying
for everything. I brought bottles of wine and made the bed.

I soaked up the taxi horns, kids laughing as they bounced a
ball along the street, garbage trucks grinding below the
window, distant sirens. With the little kitchen window open,
sounds from the inner courtyard of the building reverberated
upwards—a dog barking, the janitor hauling out the trash, rain
pelting the hard city surfaces. It was a change from the still
darkness of my Montclair property. I loved living in my little
forest, but spending time in New York brought back my
carefree days there as a young woman, only this time I wasn't
lonely. My delight was as much New York as it was Benjamin.

Benjamin had a successful career, maintained his
apartment well, had good relationships with his children, and
was sexually lively. In our occasional evaluations of our
relationship, I said I didn't want to make any commitments
because I wanted to be free to date other men. I didn't tell him
how glad I was that we were not meeting in my house, where I
would have to explain phone calls from other men. Lila called
every morning and most evenings when I was there, and those
minutes became like an empty hole in our time together—
something we acknowledged but did not talk about. We
provided comfort, amusement, regularity, and sex for each
other, and that was enough.

Several months into our demi-cohabitation, Benjamin
revealed that he had once stayed with a Danish couple with
whom he'd shared sex. He said that when the wife came to
New York, the husband gave her permission to have sex with
Benjamin, but never alone, so they went to a sex club, and he

said he had enjoyed it, and would I like to go with him. The idea was laughable, outrageous, scary, almost insulting. But he kept bringing it up, and, as had happened before with sexual subjects, repetition made it familiar. I asked him to give me some details. What did people wear, or not wear? How did people get together? What did the place look like? He patiently answered every question, then leaned his face into mine and said, "Let's go!"

Rain was thundering into the courtyard below, lashing the front windows—a hurricane was expected and the full blast hadn't even arrived yet.

"But there's a hurricane coming!"

"There will be people there. We can get a cab."

I don't know if I would have gone if the weather had been better, but finding a cab in a hurricane to go to a sex club was stupid.

The number of things we didn't talk about over breakfast was building—Lila, his teeth, his habit of turning me away from him during sex, and now my reluctance to go to a sex club.

· 35 ·

Greta Speaks

Greta wanted to meet Benjamin. "Bring him over to dinner some night."

"He doesn't come out to New Jersey."

"What kind of a boyfriend is that, who doesn't want to meet your friends, see where you live?"

"You know getting New Yorkers across the Hudson River is like getting me to Iowa."

"I've heard about that, but we're not talking about just any New Yorker."

"I get to stay in the city a couple of nights a week, and he doesn't disrupt my life at all by coming to my house. In some ways, this is perfect."

She scrunched up her face a bit and scratched her cheek. "Maybe it's just me, but it sounds like a pretty strange setup."

A few weeks later, Benjamin surprised me by offering to come to Montclair, and on a warm evening Greta, her husband Fred, Benjamin, and I had dinner together on my sun porch. The men shared their experiences in China while Greta and I served the dinner. She had brought stuffed poblano peppers and a Navajo apple pie from one of the cookbooks she had written, and I contributed cheese puffs, baked halibut, and green beans almondine.

In the kitchen afterward, Greta remarked, "He looks like somebody's husband."

After Greta and Fred left, Benjamin helped with the remaining cleanup, then said, "I understand the bus leaves at ten thirty. Would you mind taking me to the bus stop?"

He had a flare for shocking me with abrupt coldness. I had just assumed he would spend the night. I felt like shooting back, "Hah! You want to be there for your phone call from Lila tomorrow morning, don't you!" He was more afraid of her reaction than he was of my reaction if he didn't stay overnight. I took him to the bus stop. Then again, Ken had called that afternoon to ask if he could come over.

You get what you give.

· 36 ·

! ! ? ? @ # ? $ # ! ! ?

A few weeks later, I entered Benjamin's apartment to find it ablaze with candles in Scandinavian glass holders. The table was set with his finest Italian wine glasses, and he had folded the white linen napkins into bird shapes.

"Ooooh! Wow! This is lovely. Really lovely."

"It's for you, my dear."

While he put the finishing touches on dinner, I took a shower and put on his bathrobe. What was behind this surprise party? Was he going to propose marriage or tell me good-bye?

After the beet and endive salad, he told me to stay put and finished off the lamb chops and angel hair pasta, which he arranged artistically on his Spode china plates.

There were long periods of silence after my original effusions about the delicious, beautiful dinner. Suddenly he put down his fork and blurted out, "I don't know why. I'm just emotionally blocked. I can't enter into a relationship. I'm—I don't know what to say. It's just not happening."

I stayed quiet for a while. *Tell the truth*, I thought to myself. The truth was that I didn't love him either. But I had gotten used to our routine, and didn't want it to stop. This part-time relationship was plenty for me. "We've had such a comfortable time with each other."

"Yes, I know. It has been lovely having you around."

"If it's so lovely, then why do you want it to stop?"

He harked back to the miseries—the loss of his father when he was twelve, his mother's reclusive nature, his feelings of inadequacy when he felt like a hick at Harvard, Lila's illness, his sister's death, and a litany of other blows. "Maybe I'm just depressed. I don't know."

"This isn't making a whole lot of sense to me, but it takes two. If you're uncomfortable, then it has to end."

We were silent for a while, then he said, "Let's go sit on the couch and just hold each other." On the couch he cried quietly. "I can't love you, Ann. I've tried, but I can't. You're a wonderful woman and I think the world of you, but, well, I just can't."

He pleaded with me to stay the night. I was already wearing his bathrobe, and the break was abrupt. So I welcomed the chance to have it percolate overnight. Perhaps I would get a clearer explanation the next morning.

But the next morning our polite conversation filled the air with sound but little content. *Is it still raining? Did you sleep well? Is a croissant okay for breakfast? Would you like another cup of coffee?* Then I wrapped my toothbrush in toilet paper and put it in my purse. I tried not to show my confusion and anger.

He opened the door for me and said, "I'm so sorry. I don't know why this happened. I just can't. I don't know."

I wanted to keep it short. "Bye, Benjamin," I said, without a kiss or a touch, and left.

I shed a few tears over my busted up romance on the way to the subway, and as the train roared down to the bus terminal, my brain exploded in anger. *You want an upsetting past? Well how about kidnapping, divorces, being robbed of everything you own, losing your father at twenty-four, Margaret dying, being threatened with death by your spouse! I'll give you an upsetting past!!! You pussy! You weak pussy! I didn't even want you, for heaven's sake! You have lousy teeth and I don't like the way you make love to me.*

Why couldn't I see someone across a crowded room, ease into his arms for a few turns on the dance floor, and live happily ever after?

I rattled back and forth between anger and self-pity, but shucked off the extreme reaction in a day or so. This had been my first attempt at a deeper relationship, and it had failed.

The habit of Tuesday and Friday in New York was hard to break. I looked at the lights of the city from my living room, much as I had done when Bruce dumped me. I felt frustrated and disappointed, and kicked myself for proceeding with a relationship that was so obviously inadequate. Maybe inadequate was the best I could hope for. Everyone has flaws, and the older you get the more you have, or maybe the more you give up fighting them.

Benjamin seemed so upset by our parting that he would probably be in touch with me soon anyway. He had cried more than I had. I planned to move on.

· 37 ·

And Then ...

On June 22, 2004, about a month after I first met Benjamin, I checked Craigslist, where I found a posting titled "Zimbabwe coming to New York." I was intrigued and e-mailed the writer: "Tell me about it." Given the grim news about Zimbabwe that I had been reading in the newspaper, whoever was planning to come to New York had to have a good reason, and I expected that reason to occupy most of his time here. At the most, I expected a tryst shoehorned into his busy schedule.

Guy was a white businessman living in the capital, Harare. Since Zimbabwe is seven thousand miles from Montclair, and we had only the flimsiest intention to meet, this could hardly be called a "relationship," but I looked forward to his weekly letters, and increasingly used this developing friendship as a yardstick.

In photographs Guy looked mischievous, with wavy

brown hair, blue eyes, a wide smile, beautiful features, 6'1", on the thin side. Every time I looked at him I melted a little. He reminded me of my matinee idol, Gregory Peck. He suited my palate perfectly. When I showed the pictures to Greta, she said, "He looks nice." I couldn't understand why she didn't find him meltingly handsome as well.

He was married, but had lived separately from his wife, Elizabeth, for more than a decade. She still lived on the family estate just east of the city, and he wrote me about helping her with taxes, fixing the water pump, and celebrating Heroes' Day, known as "Gooks and Spooks," with his family. Being married did not disqualify him; there are so many different kinds of marriage. He was blunt and honest about the legal and personal reasons why he stayed married, clear about the devotion he and his wife felt to each other as friends and parents, even if their romance had ended long ago. He felt responsible for her comfort and safety, and his letter told of frequent discussions about the well-being of their children. He had no tolerance for fairy tales and distortions about love and marriage, and in that way he reminded me of Ken. People whose backs are against the wall, the blue-collar Ken and the besieged white man in Zimbabwe, either retreat into a world of fairy tales and distortions or become hard-minded realists. The edge and courage of both men energized and excited me.

The set of criteria I had written down when I first started dating remained in place. Guy was solvent and sane. He was kind, intelligent, sophisticated, frank, and funny in that he observed and laughed at the ironies inherent in real life. As far as I knew, he did not suffer from a condition that would require nursing.

I shared with him my reluctance to marry again. I still had no yen to make anyone breakfast, wash his underwear, or deal with a new set of children, colleagues, or parents-in-law.

He wrote, *I have had a love affair with anything female since my first erection.*

Howard was dropping in every now and again. My Match.com and other dating pages were still open, and I received regular e-mails from new men. I did not tell Guy the details of my New York dalliances, but let him know that I was not prepared to take a vow of fidelity to anyone. Since he had been getting in trouble since he was a teenager over his weakness for "anything female," I got the impression that my attitude was a novelty and a relief to him.

Loving him might be perilous; he gave a lot, but also took away. I would never be close enough to him for long enough to love him, though I was becoming increasingly dependent on his e-mails, his counsel, his opinions, and his example.

He was wrestling alive a new business, and besides the usual concerns with staff, equipment, and financing, he had problems with corrupt government officials, scarcity of diesel fuel, electricity outages, and unpredictable inflation.

He thought that in the US he might be a Republican, but the politics in both of our countries were so screwed up that it wasn't worth spending any personal capital on, and the principles he lived by were not at odds with mine. Besides, I would never meet this man.

· 38 ·

Snap! It's Serious

$\mathcal{I}$ got a longish e-mail every Sunday, sometimes more often, from Guy, written with his two index fingers. I put him in the same friendly, supportive, untouchable category as my regular e-mail correspondent Pete, until one Sunday in August when nothing arrived. I was unexpectedly bereft, and I wrote him a chiding e-mail on Monday.

He wrote right back that *the electricity had been cut the night before for 6 hours,* and: *Don't worry, darling.*
I replied:

I will remember that the way to get you to call me darling is to be fractious and piqued.

He answered:

Don't get shot away. Darling is the first name of all of my female friends.

The next week he wrote that he didn't have the funds and energy to start a new business, support his family, and start a serious relationship, and that I shouldn't consider marrying him. If anything, I had over-assured him that I was not interested in marriage, and his letter suggested that he considered my assurances nothing more than female manipulation. The more I thought about it, the more offended I became, and I fired off an e-mail:

I wasn't actually going to marry you, not quite yet anyway. Besides, you are ensconced behind the protective wall of marriage, in a nice, cozy spot. You have the best of excuses not to get married to anybody else. So keep your wedding ring.

The next morning I found his response:

My darling: It was a throw away line. Will write later, just had to tell you that your perception is not right.

Love, Guy

He had signed it *love!* If this had been a paper letter I would have clasped it to my breast.

He was upset when the deteriorating situation in Zimbabwe caused him to cancel his trip to New York. So was I. If we didn't meet each other, this connection would peter out, so I suggested that I come to Africa.

He replied:

You can come live with me whenever.

Though I was a hardened veteran of the romantic wars, this response warmed me through and through.

Our e-mails turned to planning the visit, and we settled on the first three weeks in February, which would be summer in Zimbabwe. Then he wrote about things he thought I should know before boarding the plane; for example, he had diabetes. He said that he had been diabetic since he was seventeen and had type 1 diabetes, which he told me was more easily controllable than type 2 diabetes. He said it did not interfere with his everyday life, he just needed insulin with every meal. I was not sure what to make of this revelation. He went on to say that it had made him more or less impotent: *I've had more use of the damn thing than most diabetics, maybe twenty years more, but it's finally gotten to me.* He was unable to give me the very thing that had led me to date in the first place. What more weird twists could there be?

In the same e-mail he reminded me that while he saw this as a *romantic relationship,* he had *absolutely no intention of setting up a permanent exclusive relationship. That may change over time, but right now that is how I see myself.* I didn't have the intention of setting up a permanent exclusive relationship either, but I wanted to touch him, smell him, hear his voice. He was giving me every chance to back out, and was clearly thinking about backing out himself, but his *absolutely no intention* was qualified with *That may change over time.*

I was confused and hurt by his e-mail. I thought about it for a couple of days and discovered no impulse to cancel the trip. I wouldn't sacrifice the support and stimulation of his presence in my life because of his cold feet and what he referred to as his *limp dick.*

I couldn't figure this out through e-mail. I'd go to Zimbabwe.

· 39 ·

The Safety Valves

As my feelings for Guy grew deeper, I welcomed the protective diversion of my other men. Though he was engaged to Elaine, Ken came by from time to time. His stolid, down-to-earth reactions challenged me to stay real. Howard showed up from time to time too. We had wonderful conversations, and he revealed depths I had never imagined. Sometimes we didn't even have sex.

In October, six weeks after my breakup with Benjamin, I sent him an e-mail bearing my congratulations when his beloved New York Giants won a football game and was glad when he wrote back. Our breakup had seemed abrupt, and it felt good to be friendly. He surprised me by replying that he missed me, and we reestablished our comfortable Tuesday and Friday routine, but I did not trust that relationship and told him that I was seeing other men. I didn't tell him specifically about the correspondence with Guy, which had then lasted four months, but when we made plans for my visit to Harare, I told Benjamin I was going to visit a friend in Zimbabwe, and I think he assumed it was a man, though he never asked for details.

There was another intriguing relationship unfolding at the time, one from which I truly expected nothing; that is, I wasn't mouthing to myself that I was expecting nothing, as I was regarding Guy—I truly expected nothing.

The same day that I found Guy's posting on Craigslist—June 22, 2004—I also responded to a posting by Robert, a married, fifty-seven-year-old man from London, England who planned to come to New York on business once a month. He was the editor of a magazine, and they were expanding into America.

We are such animals—we all behave the same when it comes to biological matters. Like female horses, humans, or elephants, I would recoil when a man advanced on me aggressively. I had to agree (or not). Female mammals need a little convincing—at least I do. I have concluded that most men just need to know that a woman won't ridicule them sexually before they start talking for real. The marvelous human intellect and complex human languages provide an interesting veneer, but a person is foolish to forget that the body and mind are programmed biologically. Robert's e-mail was no different from any of the other e-mails—he wanted to know if I thought we would make love when we first met. I answered, *Maybe, if we like each other.* Then the conversation began.

Robert's photographs showed a handsome man—a soft straggle of brown hair on his forehead, a shy smile, soft eyes, handsome contours, full mouth slightly open in an innocent smile. The full-length photo showed all six feet two inches of him. We both liked sports, he loved *Edvard Grieg's gloomy misty Norwegian melodies which are perfect for Scots like me who find bagpipes boring.* He couldn't dance (Why is it so difficult to find

a man who dances!?), was not religious but had a nagging fear
of reincarnation, and felt lucky because he had been successful
despite a truncated education. He wrote that he was a *true idiot.*

I wondered, *How, after all your success, did you get so self-
effacing and unconfident? Did you have an unhappy childhood or
something?*

He confessed to a long history of alcoholism, but went on
to a much more disturbing tale. When his mother committed
suicide in his twenties, he bought lingerie just like what she
used to wear, laid it out neatly on a hotel bed, took a bath, and
then put it on. He remembered every detail—the suspender
belt (garter belt), the cream and beige coloring, silk, lace. He
looked at himself in the mirror, *achingly aroused, also disgusted,*
and had the most powerful orgasm of his life. He wanted to
know which was worse, being an alcoholic or dressing up in
ladies' lingerie.

I answered:

*I'd prefer to have a man doll himself up in lingerie every
night than come home drunk.*

He went on that his mother had dressed in front of him
and he had loved gazing into the secret curves and shadows.

I thought about it during the train ride home, and wrote
him again as soon as I arrived:

*I'm kind of blown away by this. It leaves me angry with
your mother for dressing in front of you, but it's all a
grand cycle of despair.*

It was now almost midnight in London but he wasn't
done. He wrote that she had become the model for what he
desired, and that he would have made love with her given the
opportunity. I was fascinated that his pattern of desire had
lived on, as if it were a living shadow of his mother. He wrote

that this was the first time he had ever discussed this with anyone, which put a heavy burden on me.

If we had met in person, we would never have had this conversation so soon after meeting. Like Malcolm, who would not have told me how much he wanted to put his hands in my panties if we had met at a party, Robert would not have told me about his mother over cocktails. Only the Internet made it possible to share such things without fear. It was stunning how quickly anonymity and distance from each other erased inhibitions.

Robert wrote of his *abject need,* of his *unbearable tension and desire* as he imagined our meeting. I was *My darling Ann, My beloved, my love.* He wrote, *I have traced the photographs of your body with my fingertips a hundred times this weekend, dear Ann.*

The prospect of having such an open, poetic sexual partner was tantalizing, but it also felt dangerous. A few days later, he asked if I would let him try on my lingerie.

He would be gravely disappointed by my lingerie. All attempts at lacy underwear were ripped to shreds in the washing machine, and I tended more toward the practical. I wrote him what I thought was a brutal answer, ignoring the romantic tone of his e-mail on purpose:

> *With all the starving children in Africa and the bombing in Iraq, and AIDS and all the other miseries of the world, what do I care if you wear my underwear?*

He didn't respond to my flippancy, instead asking how I would dress him.

Dressing men is not my game. The rhythm of our exchange had veered off somewhere. I could envision myself in a New York hotel room with a man putting on my underwear and suffering a psychic break.

I knew what that looked like. After my second husband,

Tom, had been depressed for about a year, we drove together to drop off my son at birthday party. Driving home, Tom began muttering that we had to go back to save him from people who were "coming to get him." My son would be acutely embarrassed if his stepfather blew into his party ranting about how unidentified men were going to take him away, and I refused to turn around. Back home Tom paced back and forth, his face becoming bright red, sweat pouring off him. I took him to the hospital where the psychiatrist said this was a psychic break. I never wanted to see that again.

My feelings for Robert were sincere but not deep. His fate was tied to his own family, and did not endanger my heart.

· 40 ·

Risking Everything

My heart was in danger when I boarded the plane in Newark Airport on January 31st, 2005 on my way to Harare, Zimbabwe.

When she learned about my trip, my friend Jane sent me a poem she had written on a Kenya safari about the entrancing danger of night-howling animals that would kill and eat you. There were no such animals where I grew up. She wrote of the light, the earth more ancient than history, the grace of the people, the violence, the beauty. I thought of Hemingway, *The African Queen*, the slaughters in Biafra, the Congo, Rwanda. I remembered the gracious wife of a British Embassy official I had known in Greece who had lost half of her jaw to a rare African disease. The music, the rhythms, the politics, the history—they didn't fall into something I could easily understand, and I was ready to learn.

My seat mate from London to Harare, Lynne, was a pink,

curly-haired, middle-aged farm woman from near Gweru, several hours by car from Harare. She was returning from London, where she had put her mother into a nursing home. After takeoff she looked at me over the empty seat between us and twinkled, "We got lucky."

There was a soft ball of fat between Lynne's waist and her legs, and she couldn't fold herself into half of the empty seat, so I was the lucky one. I folded my feet up into the empty seat, nestled my head on my jacket, and slept.

After sleeping for several hours, there was still plenty of time to talk to Lynne. She grew weepy and nostalgic as we approached Harare. "Now that I've sorted out my mother, we've got to sort out our home. We've just been booted out." The "oo" came close to the French "u." Her eyes filled with tears as she repeated it, "Just booted out. We love it here, you know. We hate to go. We hate to go. I can understand their taking the farm, but I think we should be reimbursed for it. We hate to go. I can't stop saying that, can I? 'I hate to go.' I keep repeating it because maybe our leaving will become real to me that way." Confiscation of white farms in Zimbabwe felt different face-to-face.

She didn't seem angry, just grief-stricken. "The farm's being split between four people. One of them we've known for years, a very nice man, a dairy farmer."

"This is probably a stupid question, but is he black?"

"Of course, yes. I guess that's the point, isn't it. He's been very kind. He gave us until the end of February to clear out. We have to leave the farm implements, all the cattle and animals, the farm machinery, and of course the farmhouse." Her lip quivered. "We can only take our personal effects. We've lived there since 1972, first me, then my husband and children. Now they've taken it. We knew it was coming. But we love it there and we hate to go."

"What are you going to do?"

"We're going to work in a dairy in England. At least, my husband is."

"1972. That's thirty-three years."

"My first husband and I bought the farm. When the war started he had to serve every so often in the army, and another farmer's rifle went off accidentally while they were on guard duty, and he was killed. I had three young children and a farm to deal with." Lynne was calmer now.

"What did you do?" I asked her.

"My first thought was to flee. But my neighbor, a simple-minded Afrikaaner farmer, really the last person I would turn to for advice, said, 'This is the worst time for you to make a decision. You need to give yourself a year.' And I took his advice and by the end of the year things had started straightening out. I married again and stayed. I'm glad I did, mind you. We've had a good life. A very good life." Then she beamed her girly smile. "I can't wait to see my husband. You'll see him too. He'll be standing there in his shorts and his fellies, with no socks."

"What's a felly?"

"Boots. He wears them everywhere, even to church. The first thing I want to do is have some sadza."

"What's sadza?"

"The Zimbabwean national dish, made out of mealie meal." She started to giggle as she realized how lost I must be. "Mealie meal is maize, corn, what you in America call hominy, I think. They don't have sadza in England."

"At least you have a good marriage, and you'll be together."

"Oh yes. Oh yes. He's a very nice man. But all farmers in Zimbabwe are nice, do you know that?" That boded well for ex-farmer Guy.

Her two children were in South Africa and Australia. Zimbabwean families were falling asunder.

She had been generous with her story, so I told her mine.

"I'm going to meet a man in the airport whom I have never seen before, and spend a month with him."

"What! How do you know you'll like him?"

"We've e-mailed for eight months and I think I know him pretty well."

"I don't think I could do that." Her tone was confidential. "Aren't you nervous?"

"I'm supposed to be, aren't I."

"I would be."

"I'm not nervous about Guy. No, I take that back. I am nervous about Guy. Nervous that I'll fall in love with him. I've sort of fallen in love with him already, and he's married—he hasn't lived with his wife in a long time, but they are not divorced, and he lives half a world away from me. My heart might get broken."

"Honestly now, what if you don't like him?"

"I'll climb on a plane and spend a few weeks in Cape Town. This is a trip to meet Guy, but it is also a chance to see Africa. I never thought I would travel to Africa, and here I am."

Lynne started to giggle. "You've got your hands full. My hat's off to you."

I don't know why I didn't feel nuts traveling halfway around the world to meet a man who was married, diabetic, a self-described philanderer, and a potential Republican. I hadn't even asked him to share the cost of my plane ticket. Other men had been enjoyable company, but Guy's thoughts and photos had touched me as no other man's had. I needed to know what it felt like to be with him.

Our minds can no more change our attractions than the slave master can eradicate the slave's thirst for freedom. Sober intentions blow away in the hurricanes of love. Our loves are vapor. They fly. They dive. I was diving into this one headfirst.

· 41 ·

More Than I Ever Expected

Guy was standing first in line as I rolled my baggage cart out of the passenger area at 7 a.m. on February 1, 2005.

I recognized him immediately and smiled. "I know you."

"Hello, Ann," he said, and we embraced warmly, but carefully.

He was not as handsome as his pictures, but there are no pheromones in a photograph, the voice doesn't sound, the body doesn't move. He wore khaki pants made of a fine mesh material nicer than the usual, and a light blue shirt that bloused where it was tucked in. He had longish, light brown hair with streaks of grey, indifferently cut, brown eyes behind heavy glasses, a beautiful mouth and teeth, and his smooth skin was grooved from fifty-eight years of living, some of it as a farmer out in the sun. He walked with a pigeon-toed gait that reminded me of Michael Jordan. For all his good looks, he was not at all vain or strutting.

He took the airport luggage cart from me and chatted as he pushed it casually and uncomfortably. "We're really rather proud of our airport here, you know, it can stand up against the other international airports, don't you think?" The almost French "u" of his accent slipped into my ear seductively.

"It's nice."

"I don't know what you have been imagining. I hope it has lived up to your expectations so far. At least the weather is— here, let me take that for you." He reached for the smaller bag I was carrying.

I felt a tug at my sleeve, and I turned to see Lynne, my seat mate. "I just wanted to wish you luck, and to say good-bye," she said, tears springing to her eyes.

I embraced her round, warm body and kissed her cheek. Into her ear I whispered, "Good luck in your new life," and she faded away. I was so absorbed in my own adventure that I didn't even see her husband in his fellies.

Guy put my suitcases in the rusted, uneven bed of his truck, an open-backed pickup that looked like a Chevy or Ford to me, the white paint chipping, a hole in the windshield. My computer was tucked inside the cab behind the seat, and then Guy got in on the right side and reached over to unlock my door, since it would not open from the outside. There was no radio. He had a procedure for starting that required a maneuver with the key after something happened in the engine. The truck rattled as we drove off. Was this the truck of a successful businessman? What had I gotten myself into?

I felt a surprising lack of excitement as we drove down the African highway. There were no elephants or monkeys, no plains or infinite vistas.

Knowing his dislike for writing e-mails, I had stored up questions. What was his full name? Did he have any brothers or sisters? What part of Zimbabwe had he grown up in? Since he answered them easily and fully, I asked him more. What had his high school been like? Did he play any sports? The drive lasted forty-five minutes, and he seemed happy to be given things to talk about.

There was no point at which I felt we had entered a city, just homes here and there, wide roads with wide intersections, large, grassy, vacant lots, the constant stream of black Africans along the shoulder, and then he said, "This is my street. Right up there, that's my house."

The street had two lanes, with wide dirt walking paths on either side, a deep drainage trench running beside the road, tall grass, bushes, and flowers. There were fences and walls so high that I could only see the tip of the thatched or tile roofs of the houses behind them. Each compound was accessed by a steel gate.

He drove over a tiny bridge crossing the deep roadside trench, clicked a door opener, and the steel door heaved open then closed behind us as he pulled into an open metal cage with a corrugated metal roof that functioned as a garage. It was eight in the morning.

The house was a one-story, white-washed, rectangular structure with a grayish thatch roof rounding up to a point. There were occasional ivy-like green vines climbing the outer walls; they massed more thickly on the walls of the small room protruding at the other end of the house, which Guy said was the kitchen. It was almost outdoors—an intriguing prospect. The four small windows on the wall facing us had steel bars over them, and a door made of long, round steel bars stood open outside the kitchen. I could glimpse similar security provisions in all the compounds we had passed.

Guy clanged his car door shut and lifted my suitcases from the truck bed as I took my computer and a smaller suitcase from behind my seat. He led me into the kitchen, and up a small step into the living room. Curtains patterned with roses were drawn across the bow window facing on the back yard, and also across the doors in the corridor leading onto what I guessed was a terrace. I couldn't see out. The interior was dark. There was a strong, musty smell that Guy didn't seem to notice. I looked for the source and saw a stain on the thin green rug. As well as we knew each other already by e-mail, we really were starting with a blank slate. I was along for the ride—a rat in my own experiment.

A couch with a flowery, feminine slipcover faced a brick fireplace, and there were two armchairs in similar slipcovers, and a plain wooden coffee table. From our e-mails, I knew that Guy's strategy for surviving in the virulently anti-white, corrupt atmosphere of the Mugabe government was to own nothing. He had written me that every curtain, slipcover, spoon, fork, and piece of furniture belonged to his landlady. His rent was one million Zim dollars a month, about a hundred US dollars.

We put down the bags and stood facing each other. I had waited so long to meet this man. I knew so much about him: his family, his business, his children, his hopes for the future, his finances, his pleasures, his brilliance, his health, his character and personality. Now here he was. I moved forward to lay my head on his shoulder. "Isn't this just amazing?"

The strong tremor in his hands robbed his embrace of power as he pulled me to him and kissed me. Considering how diabetes had compromised his sexual potency, the tremor might have been a sign that he was feeling apprehensive when he said, "Let's get to know each other," and took my hand to lead me into the bedroom. I was not apprehensive. Maybe I should have been, but I was not. We had agreed in our e-mails that sex would be part of our relationship, so why wait? At that moment there was no place I wanted to be more than in Guy's bed. We would have so little time together.

When I took off my clothes and smiled at him he looked me up and down, and up and down, and said, "Lovely." I felt lovely, too. I weighed 145 pounds, had been swimming thirty laps every day for months, and was in great condition.

We had both been looking forward to this moment for a long time, and the affection and intimacy of our first lovemaking was so concentrated that I barely noticed any problems.

Afterwards, we were relaxing on the bed, talking and enjoying our first hours together, when I heard the kitchen door open at the other end of the house.

I was startled. "Who's that?"

"That's Susan. The maid."

The door to the bedroom was open, and I felt exposed, though she couldn't have seen me unless she had come into the room.

"What are you going to tell her about me?"

"Don't worry about her. Susan has dealt with a thing or two in her life," he said as he got up to close the door. "I'll introduce you as Mrs. Evans." I thought it was quaint and colonial to use the term "Mrs." I soon learned that he had some other quaint terms in his vocabulary, like "homo," which I hadn't heard in decades, and "Jewboy," used as innocently as my father had used it in the fifties. "If you ever visit New York," I told him, "You'll have to get some linguistic instruction beforehand so you don't get beaten up."

I WANTED A BATH after my long plane trip. The hot water reservoir was called the "geezer." When it refilled, it made a sound like a didgeridoo for ten to fifteen minutes. Once the geezer (maybe "geyser?") was full, the hot water ran fast. The cold water sometimes cut off suddenly, or ran in a trickle if the neighbors were also using water. There was a shower, but given the unpredictability of the cold-water mix, it was inadvisable to take one. The hot water was scalding, and if the cold water cut off suddenly, one could die.

After my bath, I went into the living room, where Susan was energetically sweeping the living room rug with a large whisk broom. A young child was sitting on the grass just outside the open kitchen door. She was Miriam, Susan's daughter.

Susan looked up to give me a pleasant smile, "Good morning, Medem." She was a thin woman in her twenties, about 5' 6" tall, with rich, dark skin and beautiful features. She came by bus every morning and stayed until 3 p.m. Monday through Friday, and until noon on Saturday. She did laundry in the bathtub after Guy and I finished our baths. She ironed, swept, washed the dishes, cleaned the kitchen floor with a wet rag, and tidied up. Guy told me to feel free to ask her to do my laundry or anything else that came to mind. "She'll probably like having something to do. As long as I have a clean shirt and the place is tidy, I never pay any attention. I think she spends part of every day watching my television."

Guy took me out for an early lunch. We sat on the stone terrace of a restaurant bordering a park where I could see people strolling in the February sun, some of them wearing colorful clothes and bright head wraps that fit my mental picture of "African." Over fried tomatoes, eggs, bacon, and toast, Guy spoke of his housekeeping concerns. "Besides sleeping, I don't spend much time there, and I'm worried that you'll be unhappy with the state of the place. You'll have to mind the carpet. If it rains you have to put buckets down because the roof leaks. Sometimes it rains so hard that the rug gets wet anyway. We've tried to repair the roof, but so far it hasn't worked." That explained the stain and the smell.

"I don't know what you will think of the kitchen" he went on. "There's not very much there. Some tea, coffee, sugar, and a few bits and pieces. I'll take you shopping this afternoon to get whatever you need."

We were interrupted by the owner of the restaurant, a petite, well turned out woman who Guy introduced as one of his oldest friends. She told Guy that she had been under pressure to sell her restaurant, and that she had finally given in and sold it the week before.

As they clasped hands and shared their disappointment I imagined what a wonderful, leafy hideaway this had been for Guy and his friends. That morning, we were the only customers.

We shopped at the "biggest supermarket in town" that afternoon. It was not unlike American supermarkets, except that some of the more indulgent of our materiel was missing. There were unfamiliar tropical fruits, and only one kind of apple, sweet potato, and tomato. Staples of our supermarkets, like half an aisle of sponges and mops, were missing. There was one kind of mop, and one kind of sponge, and some cheesecloth-like stuff called mutton cloth, which I supposed could function as a counter wipe to replace the ratty rags in Guy's kitchen.

What a sight—Guy wheeling around the cart, looking at things he hadn't thought about in years, like flour, and at his side the fledgling transient Zimbabwean who wondered what fruit that was, and where were the walnuts? Nowhere. No almonds, either. Only peanuts, which aren't nuts. Guy was good-humored and patient, showing me what he knew of the place and waiting with the carriage as I explored.

By dinner, we had both realized that we liked each other very much. I would not need to fly to Cape Town, and he could freely talk about his plans. "I wrote to you that I'd love to give you the full treatment—Cape Town, Zambia, Kariba."

It was like telling me he would take me to Wonderland. "I guess you must have thought I'd be good company."

"I wonder why." He smiled at me, and what a beautiful smile, what a lovely, winning, heartwarming smile.

"I've tried like the devil to get the boat in Kariba, but the family we share it with is going to be using it while you are here. And I'm afraid the pleasures of South Africa will also have to wait until next time."

"I'd love to see those things, but it's you I came to see, not a waterfall or the coast of South Africa."

He reached over to squeeze my hand. "If it's any consolation, we will be going to Nyanga." Nyanga was his house in the Blue Mountains, on the border of Mozambique. I was so pleased I would see it.

In his shirt pocket was what I first took to be a pen, but it was insulin. He stuck himself in the thigh before eating, diverting attention by looking elsewhere. He was matter-of-fact about his diabetes. "It is what it is," he said.

· 42 ·

Settling In

The first night, I didn't sleep well. The toilet and bathroom were separate rooms, and when I stumbled into the small toilet half asleep at 3 a.m. and turned on the light, poised on the wall was a spider as big as my hand. I had asked Guy about snakes and other animals I might find in the backyard (nothing dangerous there), but had not asked about spiders in the toilet. The spider and I looked at each other and decided we didn't much care what the other was doing. I have a fact in my head, which may not be accurate, that large spiders are not poisonous, only small ones. Whether that was the rule for Africa as well as America, I didn't know, but I proceeded under that impression.

Back in bed, I kept expecting the spider, and finally sat up and meditated for fifteen minutes, concentrating on my regular breathing until sleep came back to me.

The next morning, we established our morning custom of

reviewing the upcoming day while Guy took his bath, me sitting on the edge of the tub, he lounging in the hot water. Every day he told me about yet another scrape that one of his employees had gotten into, computer programs gone mad, contracts being negotiated, money coming in. Mostly Guy's employees cost him extra money, and mostly Guy paid. It felt a bit medieval to me—the Lord of the Manor caring for his serfs —but I knew so little of Zimbabwe. This was a fleeting first impression. My challenge would be not to mess up his routines and relationships.

The family estate required daily attention. The rest of his family was living a lot better than he was, but that was how he preferred it. It was part of his "identity," he said, to provide for the family whatever they required or wanted. There were cricket games to anticipate, and my own plans for the day—we talked about all of them over the morning bath.

Just before he left for what was always an intense day, we embraced. He rubbed his hands along my still-naked body, and we kissed. I felt deliciously vulnerable against his clothed, businesslike body.

After Guy left I wandered around the property, careful not to stray too close to the landlady's house. There was no chair, so I sat on a cracked concrete terrace step in the backyard on a soft, breezy, February summer day, with a big, big blue sky and puffy white clouds, thinking about how I would begin to *live* here, if only for a month. The trees around me were very tall and blocked the sun. There was something barren about the backyard, and it took me a while to realize there were no squirrels. The yard felt naked without them, as if it were a movie set. I wouldn't have expected them if I had been in the desert, but the climate here was temperate. There was green everywhere, and I expected squirrels.

The second day was warm and sunny, and I asked Susan how to open the outside gate. She showed me a button on the

wall next to the bathroom. I pressed it and walked quickly to
reach the gate before it rolled closed again, then started up the
wide dirt pedestrian path parallel to the road. I walked among
dozens of black Africans, feeling fragile, awkward, and
unprotected.

The white peoples' homes were so laden with security that
I couldn't help but think I might be a target, so I didn't carry a
pocketbook. My tiny digital camera was in one pocket,
120,000 Zim dollars in the other. If I were robbed, I wouldn't
expect much help from the streams of Africans walking past—
some smiled, some were hostile.

Zimbabweans drive on the left-hand side, and I looked in
the wrong direction for oncoming cars as I crossed the wide
avenue at the head of the street. I think I was nearly killed, but
only the drivers know for sure.

There were many more employees than I was used to in
the spacious supermarket. They helped me find what I needed,
fetched things for me, and answered all of my questions in -
depth. Every aisle seemed to have one or two men arranging
and rearranging the goods.

On that day they didn't have eggs but said there would be
some tomorrow. The only fish was frozen, the cuts of beef
were different from what I was used to. There were pork
chops and chicken. There was Golden Syrup and plenty of
instant custard pudding. The vegetables and fruits were fresh,
though limited, but I got everything I needed for dinner. The
young, black checkout clerks were friendly and giggly, with
each other and with me. They oohed when I told them I was
visiting from New York. My bill came to 70,000 Zim dollars,
and the clerks were far more adept than I was at dealing with
my handful of bills. As I turned to leave, the grinning checkout
clerk said, "One dollar? Can you give me just one dollar?"

"What would you do with one dollar? A dollar doesn't buy
a bean in New York," I teased him back.

He laughed.

"Besides, I don't have any dollars with me. I only have Zim dollars." Millions of them.

I walked back down Drew Road and rang the bell at the gate for Susan to buzz me in. Little Miriam toddled out the kitchen door toward me. She didn't speak, but greeted me with sharp upward thrusts of her head, raising her eyebrows simultaneously. She reached for the shopping bags, so I gave her the lightest one and she toddled it into the kitchen in front of me, starting a daily ritual.

I found out about a gym in the neighborhood and joined for the weeks I was there. Every morning after Guy left I walked to the gym, and then stopped at the supermarket on the way home. I wasn't there long enough to make new friends, but this routine gave my day the feeling of normality.

· 43 ·

Meatballs and Pie

On Guy's kitchen were a small ancient refrigerator, a stove, a single sink with a draining board next to it, a work table with a white Formica top, two bent frying pans, two oval-shaped aluminum pots to make porridge in, a few forks, spoons, and knives, a spatula, a blunt cutting knife, some glasses, and an assortment of mugs and plates. There were cans of cleanser and a spray can of "Killem" on the window ledge. What, besides hand-sized spiders, would it be used to kill? Two kitchen towels lay on the counter next to the sink, too old to ever be rid of their smell, no matter how often they were scrubbed and left to dry in the sun on the azalea-like bush just outside the kitchen door.

The freezer compartment was stuffed with plastic bags of dog food. Susan, I later learned, made money on the side selling dog food.

I had bought the ingredients for meatballs with white

sauce, rice, stir-fried cabbage with onions, peppers, and apples, and a peach/nectarine pie.

There was no mixing bowl, so I cut up the onions and put them in one of the tall, oval aluminum pots used for making Guy's morning porridge. I added the ground beef, soaked two slices of bread in milk in another aluminum pot, added nutmeg I found in the cupboard, salt, and pepper, mixed them all together, and formed meatballs.

I dredged the meatballs in flour, poured oil into the frying pan, and added the meatballs, then splashed in some wine from a bottle Guy had bought the day before, let it cook down, threw in some milk—and voilà, meatballs with cream sauce.

The chilled wine bottle would serve as a rolling pin, but I had no pie plate! I had never cooked in a kitchen without a pie plate. Did people in Zimbabwe make things that an American would call "pies?" One of the frying pans would serve, but it had a handle that might melt in the oven. The kitchen and bedroom drawers did not yield a screwdriver to take the handle off, so I walked to the landlady's gate where a workman was making a repair and asked him if he had a screwdriver.

"No, Medem." He was polite, but offered no solution. I could not imagine a workman getting a job done without a screwdriver, so I came at it a different way. I got the frying pan from the kitchen and showed it to him. "I need to put this pan in the oven, and I would like to take the handle off before I do." I accompanied my words with pantomime, not sure if his monosyllabic responses belied a lack of English.

He picked up a thick wire that had a diagonal cut at the end and unscrewed the handle for me. As I carried the pan back to the kitchen, I reflected on my pampered status in this world. *You are so damned civilized,* I thought to myself, *with a tool for this and a tool for that, and specialized baking implements, and yet it is all so simple.* I could live perfectly well with one-tenth the paraphernalia that surrounded me in the US, though I really missed plastic wrap.

The nectarines and peaches were juicy. I cut them up, added some sugar, nutmeg, and a little flour, and left them to sit for a while, floured the top of the Formica table, and took the opened bottle of wine out of the fridge, securing the cork well. The wine inside made it heavy, an excellent rolling pin indeed.

The pie looked quite fancy, with a lattice across the top. When I opened the oven door, air blasted out—much too hot. My translation of Fahrenheit to Centigrade had obviously been way off. I turned down the heat and hoped for the best.

The kitchen sat one step down from the rest of the house, opening directly onto the lawn, with no steps or other separation except a stone just outside the Dutch door. I opened the top half of the door for ventilation and light—and to enhance my feeling that I was cooking in a lean-to—then turned to wash the dishes.

The workman who had taken the handle off the frying pan knocked on the half-open door.

I smiled at him. "Hello again."

"Hello, Medem. Electric stopped. Fifteen minutes," he said. "Fifteen minutes."

"Can we check the fuses?"

"Yes, Medem." I didn't know if he understood me.

We walked together to the far side of the house, where a fuse box lay half hidden in ivy. The fuses were larger and differently shaped from ones I was used to. I looked at it quizzically.

"One minute," he said.

The neighbor's handyman, who spoke English very well, came back with him. He was downright jovial. "Good afternoon, Medem. We have no electricity!"

"So I see."

"He needs fifteen minutes to fix the gate, then you will have electricity again."

"Do you think that using the stove and his electric tools was too much for the electric service we have?"

He and the workman consulted on the subject in the Shona language. Their demeanor toward each other was full of banter and gestures.

"Yes, Medem. If you don't use the stove for fifteen minutes, he will have it fixed."

"Okay. Thanks a lot."

Two and a half hours later the workman finished his job. There was plenty of time to get the pie cooked. The meatballs were already done.

When Guy came home he opened the kitchen door and exclaimed, "What wonderful smells!"

He took me in his arms and kissed me warmly. "How was your day? You obviously got to the supermarket."

"I went shopping, sent e-mails, took a nap, the electricity went out, and I made dinner."

"You walked?"

"Yes. How else could I get there? It was nice."

He carefully poured beer into tall glasses, tipping them sideways so the foam would not spill over the top. "Castle beer. The best we've got." As we sat down he continued, "I'm sure you noticed that not many people walk around like that."

"I was the only white person. Do you think it's dangerous for me to walk around?"

He tilted his head, thoughtful for a moment. "It's your choice. Just keep your eyes open."

He settled with a tired sigh onto the couch and I curled up in the armchair, wondering if he had even noticed that I had opened the curtains to let sunlight into the room. "The electricity went out? You should call me if something like this happens."

"I wanted to take care of this without bothering you."

"That's very sweet of you, but you shouldn't hesitate."

"Do you know what happened with the gate? Why were they repairing it?"

"They tried to breach it last night. They were looking to take the motors, which are worth a lot of money. But fortunately they only made of mess of the job and left some repairs."

"Who is 'they'?"

"It would be nice if we knew so we could send 'them' to jail, but for the moment they are just 'they.' I used to have a lovely stereo. I'd come home on a winter evening and sit right here in front of the fire, have my whiskey, and listen to music, but that was all whisked away by 'them'."

He sat at the table and poured the wine from the rolling pin into our glasses as I put the plates on the round table covered with a tablecloth with roses on it. He held his fork in midair and studied his plate. "You made this in *my* kitchen?"

"I've cooked in worse."

"Unbelievable. I've lived here for six years and I've never had a meal at this table. I've had the odd steak or hot dog, some breakfast eggs and bacon, but never a real dinner, and this looks absolutely delicious."

"Then I hope you like it."

"You are wonderful, my dear. Absolutely wonderful." He squeezed my hand before taking the first bite.

After dinner we lingered at the table. "There's one thing I want to tell you about, just in case it ever happens," he began. "If I ever start acting peculiar, slurring my words or acting drunk, please give me some sugar. You know I'm diabetic and that might happen some time, so I want you to know and not to get worried. It's hypoglycemic shock. If I get to the point where I'm slurring words, then I might be past the point where I would get the sugar myself."

"Okay." It seemed pretty simple. No alarm bells went off; I was receiving so much from him it seemed a trivial task to keep my eye on him.

I had already begun to fall in love with Guy through our e-mails, and as I looked at him over the dinner table, seeing how he appreciated everything I was doing for him, I fell more in love with him. He was handsome, sharp, clear, easy to be with, substantial.

Though he professed not to be "touchy feely," he was wonderfully affectionate, and we curled up together to go to sleep. He said quietly into my hair as we lay waiting for sleep to take us, "No woman has ever spent the night here."

I broke out of his embrace and turned to give him a sharp look. "You said you'd had lots of girlfriends."

He grinned. "I didn't say that no other woman had ever been in this bed, just not overnight."

I snuggled back again, wondering what those other women had thought of the lumpy mattress. "Isn't it lovely," I murmured.

· 4 4 ·

9 1 1

started awake with the feeling that something was wrong. The bed was moving. Were there earthquakes in Harare?

"Guy," I whispered.

He didn't answer.

"Guy?" I said it more loudly.

In the faint light from the moonlit corridor, I could see his mouth pursed, his head thrashing from side to side, his fists clenching, his whole body tense. "Guy, Guy, can you hear me?" His eyes were open and looking at me, but there was no focus or response in them. His breath came loudly and quickly through his nose.

"Guy what's going on?" I gently shook his shoulder. I thought he was dying. I had no idea where either the hospital or the telephone book were. Did they have ambulances in

Harare? What was their 911—if they had one, which I doubted? If he didn't respond to me, I would open the kitchen door—but where was the key, it was locked from the inside—no, I would call out the window until somebody came from next door to help.

The can of condensed milk on the refrigerator door! I ran to the kitchen to get the milk and a spoon.

I sat on his side of the bed and fed him a small spoonful, which he eagerly grabbed with his lips. His eyes were not communicating and his head was still thrashing. I waited to be sure that he could take it all right, then gave him another spoonful.

When the can was empty, I got a washcloth from the linen closet and wet it. His body was sweating, struggling, only less violently. He smelled like an athlete after a marathon. I wiped his face, his neck, his hands with cool water, speaking to him constantly.

His body gradually relaxed, his breathing became regular, and he lapsed straight into sleep without acknowledging me. I watched every whisker, every eyelash, as he settled back, exhausted after a struggle for life.

I washed my hands of the sticky substance and came back to bed, but couldn't sleep. He did not seem to be in a coma, but I didn't want to go to sleep until I was sure he would be all right, so I sat up, crossed my legs, and started to meditate. I did my best to make my breathing the only thing that existed in my world, and slowly its rhythm quieted me.

"What are you doing?" I was startled to hear from behind me, clear as a bell.

"Calming myself down."

"Oh." He turned over and went back to sleep.

The next morning he had to brace himself on the back of a chair on his way to the toilet. He patted my thigh as he got back into bed. "Good morning."

He didn't mention the attack, and when I asked him about it he closed his eyes in a painful frown. "Fuck!! Shit. To inflict this on you. It's inexcusable."

"You couldn't help it."

"I know, but I didn't want to inflict this on you." His head sank to the side in frustration. He breathed out forcefully through his nose.

"Does this happen often?"

"I don't remember them so I can't say how often. If you hadn't just told me I wouldn't ever know, except that I feel a little woozy just now."

"It was kind of scary."

"I'm so sorry." He stroked my arm.

"I used the condensed milk in the kitchen."

"You did just the right thing. The one thing you have to keep in mind is that I always come out of it in the end. The body starts to get its sugar from fat. It's a hell of a way to fix things, but it has always worked for me, so far anyway."

"Looks to me as if you could die from this."

"Every time it happens I lose a million or so brain cells. But we have billions. The doctor who first diagnosed me, a long time ago, was also diabetic. He warned me that I could keep the sugar levels in control with insulin, but that just one of these attacks could wipe me out. I'm counting on living to about eighty, as he did."

I thought I might like knowing him for the twenty-two years that would pass before he was eighty.

· 45 ·

Out and About in Harare

A few days later, Guy took me to a sadza restaurant, Roots of Africa, for lunch. The roof of the restaurant was grass, tiles on the floor, the seats of the carved wooden chairs upholstered with yellow-and-black-patterned cloth. A middle-aged black man absorbed in eating his sadza was the only other person there.

The waitress brought a bowl of warm water and a pitcher, and poured water over our hands before we began. "You eat sadza with your fingers," Guy explained.

The sadza was a mound of smooth mealie meal. It was, as Lynne had said, like hominy. My sauce, or "relish," was a chicken thigh and wing, and Guy had a whole fried fish from Kariba and chopped up tomatoes and kale.

We made balls of the mealie meal with our fingers and dipped them in sauce or scooped up chicken or kale. It was delicious, and messy. Our beer glasses got sticky. After we finished, the waitress again brought around a bowl of warm water, only this time it was soapy. She poured this over Guy's hands, then my hands. We shook our wet hands and rubbed them against our pants, then five minutes later she came around with a bowl of clear water to wash off the soap, and a towel.

"Why don't you provide a towel every time?" Guy asked.

"Because people take them," she explained apologetically.

We got up from the table and Guy whispered into my ear, "You'll notice that I was served first. The men come first around this place."

We sat in the sun on a low wall outside the restaurant afterward, waiting for his assistant, Lovemore, to pick us up. "We're being truly African now," I remarked, "sitting outside on the street waiting for something to happen."

MY DAILY WALKS BROUGHT me into contact with a part of the Zimbabwean world I wasn't learning about through Guy. I passed dozens of people every day, and every once in a while I would fall into conversation with one. I couldn't help noticing that there were no old people. The only old black man I had seen was the landlady's gardener. So this was what a country looked like when the average life expectancy was in the forties.

One day a black African woman of about thirty greeted me and asked if I needed a cook. She had experience with American cooking, "especially fried chicken." I told her I was only visiting, and we continued our chat about cooking for a while, then she fell away.

Another day, a scruffy-looking white man on a bicycle greeted me as he made a wobbly turn to get around me. A very short black man with terribly bloodshot eyes scurried up behind me. "Why is that white man begging? Do you know he stopped me and asked me if I could help him?" The man was astonished and couldn't contain his laughter.

I smiled. "You should see New York City. There are thousands of white beggars there."

"Really?" He was again astonished.

"Maybe he's crazy?" I suggested.

The man thought that was very funny, then changed the tone of his conversation. "It is very hard here right now," he said. "Very hard. There is not enough rain and we cannot get mealie meal. And you know in Zimbabwe we eat only mealie meal."

It was hard for me to comprehend that a person could feel so bereft without sadza. "You would have to eat something else, I guess, right? Potatoes or vegetables, or peanuts or eggs or something?"

"Our stomachs love only mealie meal."

We walked along in silence for a while, then he continued speaking, "Life is very hard here now. The only way I can get ahead is if I have rand or dollars. Could you help me? Could you give me some rand, or some dollars?"

I only had Zim dollars for groceries in my pocket, but would have given him something if I had not felt that I was constantly being watched. I thought it would be dangerous to show that I was carrying money and was willing to give it away. The word would get around very quickly among the hundreds of black Africans who walked up and down Drew Road every day. "I'm very sorry, but I don't have much money in my pocket, and besides, I only help people I know, and I don't know you."

He changed the subject abruptly but pleasantly. "What is that? Is it a phone? What is it?"

"It's a camera."

A truck roared by and I couldn't hear him clearly, but could make out the subject matter of his next conversational foray, Jesus God. If I helped other people then Jesus God would smile on me. Jesus God was watching. After the truck passed, he ended his little sermon with, "You say you don't know me. My name is Innocent."

I was glad that we had reached the supermarket. Refusing help to someone in such dire need was very uncomfortable. "I have to go shopping over there. I wish you a lot of luck, Innocent."

"Good bye, Medem."

He seemed to have no hard feelings.

· 46 ·

The Sweep of Zimbabwe

O n Friday morning, we left Harare and drove along the two-lane highway, climbing all the time.

When we stopped at a small shopping center in the town of Rusape for some weekend provisions, Guy asked me to stay in the car to guard it. As he parked, a young man came over and leaned on the driver's side window, "You want me to watch your car, sir?"

"You mean so you won't steal it?" Guy parried.

"No boss. So somebody else doesn't steal it," the young man good-humoredly parried back.

Guy smiled as he opened the door and the young man rejoined a group loitering on the corner. I admired the young man's enterprise in this mostly unemployed country.

Back on the road, we passed three women at an intersection stirring laundry with a wooden stick over a wood fire, and, a few miles later, groups of white-garbed members of a religious sect called "Apostoli" having what looked like church services.

Open trucks packed with black African men passed us. At the side of the road lay the abandoned, still-smoking carcass of an aged bus, and we wondered whether all the passengers could possibly have escaped the conflagration.

Suddenly, there was a roadblock ahead of us, with soldiers standing at either side of a gate stretching halfway across the road. Guy quickly instructed me, "Pull down your seat belt to make it look as if it works, and don't say anything. It's nothing to worry about. They're not looking for people like us." I pulled the broken seat belt down with my left hand, and held it against the seat. They waved Guy through.

We passed baboons playing on a railroad track and Guy pointed out a high ridge where a few weeks before he had seen a herd of kudu silhouetted against the sky.

There were thatched Shona huts along the road, but I had no feel for what life was like in them. I wanted to savor my time with Guy. The way of life inside Shona huts could wait for some other time. If there was one . . .

Guy's Huguenot family had arrived in South Africa in the 1600s, the same time my family was arriving in America. They farmed in South Africa, then moved to Southern Rhodesia at the beginning of the 20th century. Until Robert Mugabe came to power seventy years later, his family had been part of a hard-working, tightly knit farming community.

Sere fields that had once been the pride of southern Africa now lay idle. Plastic coverings over acres of empty greenhouses shredded in the wind. Private game parks lay empty of animals, which Guy said had been "run off or shot." Streams of black Africans trickled steadily along both sides of every road. The unemployment rate was set at 70 percent, though I wondered what the definition of "unemployed" was. Was the man at the side of the road repairing bicycles with two ancient tools "unemployed?"

In the complex that now stood empty, a brilliant agronomist had developed a strain of wheat that thrived on the light cycles and seasons of Zimbabwe. As Guy explained, "You can't throw down seed corn that grows in Kansas and expect it to thrive in Zimbabwe." The agronomist had long ago left for Australia.

The road passed through Guy's former property, and he pointed out the tiny sliver of white foundation on a hill—all that remained of the house that had been "mortared to the ground" in the 1970s. Fortunately, nobody was home, not even the farm manager. The seven attackers had tried to escape to the mountains, five were killed, and one of Guy's neighbors had taken a bullet in the shoulder, partially disabling him for life.

We pulled over and got out of the car. "When you were a farmer, did you ever stand up there in your house on the hill and survey your little empire?"

"Every once in a while. Not often."

"And do you miss your connection to the earth and all that?"

"I was never interested in that side of it. I just looked at it and said, 'How much money can I make out of this land?' Whoever has it these days isn't making any. You see that dam over there? You remember I told you that I set up an irrigation system on my pastureland? Well, the dams are still there, but fuck all is happening. Hard to imagine that there were cattle, dairy cows, maize, a whole host of crops on this land, and not too long ago. All idle."

We stood for a while, soaking up the vista. The hills rolled with a soft green cover of grass. There were acacia trees, gum trees, and who knows what those other trees were. Unlike Guy, every morning the roll of the hills to the distant mountains would have soothed my soul.

We were silent as we drove on. It wasn't so much his love

of the land that caused Guy's sadness and regret; it was the lifetimes of blood and sweat that had soaked into these lands, the shame that all of that was now wasted. He pointed out the former farms of his parents, his parents-in-law, his brother-in-law, friends, old lovers. All gone.

A blended English/Afrikaaner way of life took shallow root in the ancient African soil, bloomed for a while, and now was gone. If I had been an unconnected tourist, how could I have known what these places used to be?

As we entered the National Trust land, Guy told of his time in the intelligence service of the Rhodesian army during the 1970s rebellion. He and a female colleague, Philippa Berlin, traveled from village to village, hut to hut, talking to the Shona villagers to find out whom they were going to vote for: Musarewa or Mugabe. Guy was fluent in Shona, but Philippa was more than fluent. She also had a genuine interest in the villagers, and they had warmed up to her. The white authorities were expecting Musarewa to win, and that was what the villagers first told them, but after a while they revealed that the whole village was voting for Mugabe. When Guy and Philippa wrote their reports, their white superiors did not believe their conclusions.

Knowing Guy, I asked if he and Philippa were lovers. She was married, but so what. He said that for once in his life, no, they were not lovers. He spoke of her with reverence and said he still grieved her death in a plane crash several months after they finished their work.

We drove up the winding mountain roads, past a forest thick with acacia trees, their umbrella-like shapes shading the road and clumped together in nature's sculpture garden. Even there, miles from anything, there were people walking along the road.

The last stop was at the Pungwe River. We turned off the highway and bumped and shivered down a terrible road. At the bottom was a tiny guardhouse, and Guy got out to speak to the uniformed guard lounging in front of it. They chatted and laughed in Shona for a while, then Guy got back in the car and confirmed that the guard had a lonely job. Day after day went by with not a single visitor.

We drove to the river, where two cottages stood, one on each side of the ford. The far cottage was partially obscured by six-foot weeds. According to the park warden, everything had been stolen from the cottages—the solar panels on the roof, the refrigerators, everything. There was only one blanket left in them, no other amenities, and no tourists.

Guy stood at the side of the river and reconstructed the spot. "Best trout fishing in Africa right here. People used to reserve two years in advance to stay in these cottages. I'd like to fix them up and rent them out. But that road. Impossible to get down here. And really, there's nothing left. Except maybe the trout."

We bumped and shivered back up the road, past hillside after hillside of neatly planted pines waiting to be harvested, past the sawmill, past the always-present Africans walking the roads, some of them hitchhiking, some carrying parcels, some just walking purposefully. This is what the whole world used to be like before the automobile.

As we pulled into the gravel parking area above Guy's house, a black African with a deformed right arm came out to greet us.

"Hello Chikupa," Guy said. "Did you get the grass mowed?"

"I'm just doing it now," he replied, and spun around to get the lawn mower.

"He just got out of jail for beating his wife," Guy offered as we got out of the truck.

The maid, Rainier, had laid the wood and lit the fires for the geyser, the living room fireplace, and the stove, where I would cook all our meals for the weekend.

We put down our bags and took two cold beers onto the back terrace, where we spread ourselves out in wide wicker chairs and watched the sun set over Mount Inyangani in Mozambique. The extravagant African sky offered zigzags of aqua, cerise, and blushing clouds. The offering was so spectacular that we sat there until we were shivering, then went inside to cook dinner on the wood stove.

· 47 ·

Nyanga

I was excited about cooking dinner on the wood stove. I measured eggs, milk, and sugar with a bit of vanilla, poured the mixture over some bread, and put it in the oven, where it became a bread pudding. The water came to a boil for the rice, and on the iron top of the stove itself I grilled eggplant and pineapple and cooked two steaks. The fire went down too far, and Guy brought in more wood to stoke it up again. On the wood stove, I could move things around from hot to less-hot spots, put them on the ledge, where plates warmed nicely, or leave them in the warming oven. Cooking on a wood stove felt like driving with a stick shift.

The next morning the mountain mists fogged distant views, and it rained heavily. Foggy phantasms sailed through the wooden fence around the herb garden, through lush glades and mountainous hydrangeas. The wood fires stoked early in the morning by Rainier were welcome and cozy.

Guy got up and ran the bath. I lazed in it as he shaved, then he lazed in it as I sat on the side of the tub wrapped in a towel. It was chilly outside the tub. We were in the mountains.

After the bath, I made breakfast. While bread toasted on the stovetop, I stood at the kitchen window looking out at the mist. Ten feet away was a bird out of a picture book, chirping in the pouring rain. It was flitting from branch to branch on a bush with bell-like red flowers hanging downward off of long stems. The tiny bird, just a tad larger than a hummingbird, had a bright yellow beak and iridescent blue wings. It clicked its beak into the center of the flowers.

Breakfast was bacon, fried tomatoes, toast, scrambled eggs, passion fruit juice, and marmalade eaten at the dining room table with a view of the formal side garden. Guy's wife was a master gardener and her touch added beauty everywhere. Then we sat in front of the fire and talked about archaeology and our children, the photographs Guy didn't have of himself from when he was young, and the hundred other things that kept us talking from noon Friday until Sunday evening when we drove back to Harare.

· 48 ·

Vastly Pampered

My routine brought back dim memories of my childhood, when my grandmother had a maid, cook, laundress, and gardener, and my parents had a maid. For the first time in many years I thought about James, the gardener; Etta, who made marvelous mashed potatoes; and Ida, who took me and my brothers to Radio City Music Hall for the Christmas show every year.

Living in Zimbabwe was like going back fifty years, to a time when black people and white people "knew their places." In America the simple fact of my white skin had given me certain privileges. I was more than willing to give up those privileges in the interest of equality and fairness, though I would be blind not to know that American society still plied white skin with privilege.

I tried to calibrate my attitude in this new situation. Zimbabwe was not America. I didn't want to offend Susan by asking her to do too much, or turn Guy's household upside down by being too chummy with her. Susan and I cooperated during the day, and I often took Miriam on my lap and let her bang away at my computer keyboard or played patty-cake and peekaboo with her. Miriam spoke no English, so I taught her a few words, the first of which was "banana."

Susan could enforce the standards I chose to set. It didn't take long to get used to this. I tried my hand at being the mistress of the household by asking her to wash the curtains.

"Really?" she said.

"Don't you think they are dirty?" I asked her gently. I had cleared my project with Guy, but wanted to be careful.

"Oh yes, Medem."

Two days later, the curtains were washed and rehung. I had suspected all along that they were white.

Susan left around three, and I relaxed and then prepared dinner until Guy came home. I was flattered that he came home earlier every night. "With you, I can leave my work behind," he said. "You're very good for me."

After all my claims that I didn't want the obligations of taking care of someone else, I was amazed at how much I loved taking care of Guy.

In our evenings together I learned things about sex that I had never known—that a man can have an orgasm without an erection, for one. Deprived of full erections, I could isolate the fact that most of the fulfillment of sex is in the shared affection, the feeling of intimacy, the touch, smell, and sound of each other. I also learned that a purely physical affliction can improve against reason when buttressed by confidence and attraction. "I feel just as I always did," Guy said, "I'm just as attracted to you, want you just as badly, but this thing just doesn't work anymore."

I learned that there is no reason to stop having sex just because erections don't come easily, or partially, or not at all.

Intimacy is pleasure, and what more intimate sharing than the knowledge of what kind of erection he got, how and when, and what he could do with it? And what more intimate for him than to discover what pleased me? The sight of Guy naked, his kisses, the brush of his chest hair against my skin, his whiskers, the sound of his voice, the warmth of his body pressed against mine as we went to sleep—my pleasure was deep.

· 49 ·

Going Deeper

Guy took me to the university for a linguistics presentation I'd arranged to make there. An overflow crowd of about forty-five people had gathered in a large, dark room—the entire linguistics department, they told me. Only one of the attendees was white, besides Guy, who stood in the very back of the room. He said he wanted to be a fly on the wall. It went very well and Guy was impressed, but commented, "I understood fuck all."

There was one week left. I was getting bored and felt caged inside the tall walls of the compound. I wrote, played with Miriam, exercised, and made dinner. I was always nervous about picking up the phone—the telephones were clunky and old-fashioned, without Caller ID. What if it was Guy's wife, or one of his children? What would I say? Guy said not to worry about it; he'd deal with it if one of them called or came by.

In the evening we watched cricket, the BBC news, and the occasional movie. I was interested in cricket but knew nothing about it, and felt no attachment to a team. Attachment to cricket was a mark of the White tribe in Zimbabwe—a tribe I could never belong to. After we had our dinner, Guy was exhausted not only from his intense, busy days, but because, although a stranger would not have seen any evidence of it, he was not well. We retired early.

The thought of parting from Guy was almost unbearable. I had never known anyone, male or female, with whom I shared a groove so naturally. But I would be a burden to Guy if I stayed, and my family and my job were in New York. Without a car I could not venture outside the walled compound except to walk to the gym and the supermarket. The place was risky and desperate and only Guy's inventiveness, intelligence, and determination made it possible to prosper there, and even t! en, the Zimbabwean definition of "prosper" was different from mine.

Benjamin ventured way out on—for him—an emotional limb, e-mailing, *I'm thinking of you, but then that's nothing new.* My feelings for Benjamin were eclipsed by Guy, but Benjamin didn't live seven thousand miles away from me, didn't have diabetes, and was not married.

One phone call was from a woman asking for Susan, who had gone to retrieve the laundry. I asked for the woman's name so I could tell Susan who had called.

"I'm Susan's aunt. Could you please tell her that her nephew has died?"

"Oh no!" Given Susan's youth, I imagined the nephew was a young child.

"Yes, it's very sad. We would like Susan to know. Tell her the funeral will be tomorrow in Mutare."

I phoned Guy to ask if he would prefer to tell her, but he said, "No, you can tell her."

"Should I give her some money for the bus fare to the funeral? The woman said the boy died in Mutare."

Guy sighed. "Oh I guess so. Give her 100,000."

I heard the door close as Susan and Miriam returned. Given the cultural undercurrents, I was not confident that I would find the right way to tell her about her nephew, but I reassured myself that people are people all over the world, and the loss of a young child has the same effect on everyone.

I went into the living room where Susan was ironing in front of the window. "I'm afraid I have some bad news for you, Susan."

She frowned.

"I'm sorry to tell you that your nephew in Mutare has died."

Her face did not change expression. "Oh."

Her blank response surprised me, so I kept talking. "How old was he?"

"Same age as Miriam. Eighteen months." She shifted Guy's shirt to iron the collar.

"I'm so sorry to hear it."

"Thank you, Medem."

"You'll need some bus fare, won't you? I will give you 100,000 dollars."

"Thank you so much, Medem. I do not have the money to go, so thank you."

"How did he die? Was he sick for a long time?"

"I don't know, Medem." I thought she was lying to me, but did not press her. With the high rate of AIDS in Zimbabwe, I wondered if that was the cause, but she had her reasons for not telling me more, and I left it at that. I understood, or thought I understood, that Susan's emotions were reserved for her own people.

I went to the kitchen to make toast, and when I came back into the living room she looked up once again from her ironing, a thoughtful expression on her face. "You are not like the others, the white women, Medem."

"Really?" Caught off guard, I became wary.

"Yes. I want to stay with you."

"You want to come to America? You and Miriam? That would be nice for me." I was searching for the right words to say. I admired her chutzpah in broaching such an impossible dream.

"Yes. I want to stay with you. The other lady doesn't like my daughter. She doesn't want her here. You are different. You are not like the others."

"Miriam is my pet. It's much more fun playing with her than playing with my cats." We laughed, including Miriam, who was beginning to answer me in short phrases of English after playing with me daily for three weeks.

Susan turned back to her ironing. "I wish you would stay."

Before leaving half an hour later, Susan knocked lightly on the bedroom doorjamb before coming into the bedroom, where I was working at my computer.

She said, "Be sure to close the windows when you go to sleep tonight. There are thieves around."

"But there are bars on the windows," I noted.

"They cut them."

"Wouldn't they also break the window?"

She shrugged. "Just be careful, Medem."

Steel gates, metal bars—how much more "careful" could a person be? I was touched by her concern. Dark things were happening around us in Harare, and she knew them even better than Guy. I was flattered that she had shown me even a sliver of what she knew; her concern made her previous comments more sincere. Maybe there was a chink in the Shona reserve. I wouldn't be there long enough to find out.

· 50 ·

Caring for Guy

ater that day, it began to rain. I had to put buckets in the living room, as the roof repairman wasn't scheduled until the next day. When I went to the kitchen to make a cup of tea, I looked into the yard and saw a river of rushing, swirling, muddy water pouring through it. I rushed outside to check where the electrical connections came into the house. They had been placed far away from the water's course, which flowed under the steel gate and along the side of the house to the property's back wall, running a foot deep in places.

There was no radio in the house, and the television weather report came from the BBC or CNN in London and was very general when it came to Harare. As had happened so many times when I was in Zimbabwe, I imagined myself living in the times before we were so tied to technology and turned my face upward to judge the situation for myself. Billows of grey clouds were jousting for position in the sky, rushing southwestward, galloping, romping, going away. This flood would play itself out, and it looked like that would be the end of it.

When Guy came home, he said, "It's wonderful having someone to organize things at home. You've done such a good job of it."

I loved taking care of Guy. I loved Guy.

Later that night I awoke to the strange hypoglycemic breathing. His mouth was pursed, his head moved sharply back and forth, his body was stiffening. I asked, "Guy, can you hear me?" and he answered, "Hmmmmm," so he wasn't too deep. I got the condensed milk and fed it to him in little spoonfuls. What was the "correct" amount?

As he came to, I said to him, in a soft voice but not sweetly, "You could go into a coma or die or something, and I'd never know."

"That's as it should be," he answered.

"You need a pretty nurse to sleep with you every night," I teased. "Maybe you could get the State to pay for it."

He laughed curiously, "The State would never pay for a nurse."

The hypoglycemic shock had taken away his sense of humor. I was learning how to deal with Guy's diabetic episodes, feeding him sugar more appropriately, spotting the signs that his sugar was low more accurately. The next morning I made him a good breakfast to steady his system. He did not remember the previous night's episode.

I wondered how happy I would be bearing the burden of his care. In the list of pros and cons that I had made at the beginning of my adventures, one of the cons was "suffering from a condition which required nursing." He never asked me for a thing, but I loved the man. I took on the job of thinking through the ways he could improve his health. Guy had barged through his life defying his diabetes. As he approached sixty, he would need to be more mindful than he had ever been if he wanted to live until eighty. He ate all the wrong things, forgot to eat, put himself under stress, and was living in a place where medical care was primitive. Deep under his personal habits was the fact that he was trying to provide for his children and his family. Nothing and nobody would ever supersede them.

I would never know the answers to those questions, because we did not have a choice. I would have to go home and take care of myself and my own family as well as I could, and he would revert to the conditions he'd lived in before I arrived.

· 51 ·

The Market

There was nothing in the way of gifts for my children and friends in the stores I frequented, so we went to the Mbare Market. Lovemore and a man he called Uncle rode in the truck bed and stayed there to guard it while we went shopping. We parked the truck on a street outside a long row of corrugated iron-roofed sheds.

I could easily have gotten lost in this maze of entrepreneurial mayhem without Guy. There were streets careering in from all directions at the nearby intersection, with no street signs. People stood in groups under trees, or in front of their stores. Deliveries were underway, repairs, closings, openings.

We went past the food section, the electronics section, past stands where they sold batteries, nails, millet meal, clothes, shoes, CDs. Guy inspected wrenches. There were people milling, sitting, sleeping, selling, chatting, laughing, singing, looking hostile, looking curious, saying good morning.

One woman was sitting cross-legged on the ground with a child about four years old standing next to her and a baby at her breast. Behind her was another mother sitting on an oil can, with her head lying on a table a couple of feet higher than the oil can, fast asleep, her child sitting quietly on the table at her head. Raw life flowed through and around that market. We went into a long shed where multiple vendors sold musical instruments, baskets, perfume bottles, jewelry, wall hangings, wood carvings, soapstone sculptures. I was among five or six buyers at most.

Only the most pure of heart could pass through the Mbare Market without realizing that if you wanted something illegal, this was the place to come. Guy had mentioned sending Lovemore here for brown sugar and a hubcap, but I got the impression that the men who were watching us carefully would know where to find anything from a prostitute to a gold bracelet to a fix of morphine.

If it was difficult to draw a bath in Guy's house, I could imagine it was far more difficult in the houses where these black Africans lived. The people smelled as anyone would smell without regular showers, deodorant, and perfumed shampoos and soaps. They smelled like the human animal that we all are. I could breathe in essence of human. I liked it.

At Mbare, I was a tiny spray of white foam on a deep black sea.

Guy exchanged quips with a group of three young men after one of them called out in Shona with a suggestive tip of his chin toward me.

"What did they say?" I asked Guy.

"They said, 'Good luck, old man.' They also told me that business was bad, very bad."

I came away with two bracelets and several African musical instruments—a Y-shaped instrument with rusty discs strung along a wire, rows of wooden knobs worn around the legs that shake out a rhythm when the feet are pounded, two tiny, decorative drums strung together with a leather thong. They represented a part of Africa that I hoped to learn about when I came back—the music. I also bought a honey-colored wood carving of giraffes, elephants, and wildebeest. This was meant for my wall, where it would remind me of one of the richest experiences of my life.

· 52 ·

The Dreaded Good-Bye

The day before I left Harare, I packed my bags. Everything felt heavy. I lay my clothes in the suitcase with reluctance. When I rolled it into the living room, I was pulling a ton of sludge.

Guy came home early in the afternoon. After dinner we lay in bed and watched an old movie starring Maureen O'Hara. There was a moment in the movie when I burst out laughing. At that moment—not slightly afterwards, not slightly beforehand —at that exact moment, Guy burst out laughing too. It wasn't an intentionally comic moment, it was a moment when we both found life itself funny in exactly the same way. We looked at each other and smiled, kindred spirits.

My plane was at five on Saturday afternoon. That morning as we lazed in bed and talked, I wanted to preserve every ephemeral word and touch. I studied his body, his face, listened carefully to his accent.

"I have thoroughly enjoyed every minute with you," he said. "I couldn't have asked for anything better—and you know, this could have been a total fuckup."

I was dogged by a feeling that this was the last time I would ever see him. "I would feel so much better if I could be absolutely sure I'd see you again. But there can be no certainty about that, I know."

He shrugged his shoulders. What could he say?

The details about my proposed August visit, like who would pay for my airline ticket, would have to wait. He was caught in a sad historical moment in Zimbabwe, and I was sitting comfortably on history's divan in the United States. It would be foolish to imagine that the financial burden could be shared equally. I couldn't worry about such things. All he could promise was that he would pay for everything once I was in Zimbabwe.

He loaded my bags into the truck and backed out of the garage. The steel gate clanged behind us as we drove over the tiny bridge spanning the drainage ditches. He turned right along the tree-lined road, driving up the same path I had walked almost every day of my visit. "Good-bye, Harare," he said.

"Don't say 'good-bye, Harare,' because I'll come again. Maybe." There was something of the fairytale about our time together. The odds of it happening again were slimmer than most.

"One lives in hope." He squeezed my knee. "It's funny what things happen. Last fall I would never have been thinking South Africa, now I am thinking South Africa. If this latest deal comes through, maybe you can come back and we can drive around South Africa looking for a nice little cottage."

"That would be lovely. If. Today I just feel like crying." The pain was terrible. I was trying not to cry hysterically, but wanted him to know the pain was there.

He reached over and squeezed my leg again, keeping his eyes on the road.

We got my bags checked and walked toward the place of parting. Two feet away from the man who would take my ticket, Guy put his arm around me, pulled me toward him, and kissed me again and again. "It's been a wonderful month. Wonderful. I'll come and see you in New York."

I kissed him again, then again. "Thank you Guy, for everything." Besides my love for him, I had seen how he'd made lemonade awash in the lemons of Zimbabwe, and this had changed the way I viewed life. I would return home with a better hold on my emotions, too, after watching the consequent, hard-edged, powerful way he dealt with his life, one day at a time.

"I'll stay here until you go past that red point," he said. I loved the way he would tell me, when he knew, exactly what was going to happen. Some things he couldn't know, and I couldn't know.

The ticket-taker gave me a sympathetic smile as I handed him my ticket. Walking toward the "red point," I was seized by dizziness. My pain became physical for a moment, and I stopped, putting my hand to my forehead, and bowed my head for a moment. I hoped I wouldn't involuntarily fall to my knees from grief. After my month with Guy I was more sure than ever that pain is not a reason to do, or not do, something. I had said all along that I would swallow the pain. It was going down hard.

I continued walking, turned, blew him a kiss. He blew a kiss back, waved, turned, and left.

The taste of his kisses faded as I flew to London. All the stores at the Harare airport had been closed. If they were closed for the daily flight to London, I wondered what could be important enough to get them open. The stores in the Nairobi airport, on the other hand, were bustling and full, and I bought two more bracelets.

In London, airplanes from most of the airlines in the world were parked at their bays. The water in the sink in the ladies' room ran fast and full. There were coffee bars where they served brewed coffee, not instant. These were the harbingers of the convenience and plenty that I was returning to. I had a strange feeling of upside downness as well—for one month I had looked at news from the other side, from underneath. It was summer in Harare, and news reports from London showed people in heavy coats. From Harare, the Middle East was up there, not down there.

I had the odd sensation of having dreamed, or fantasized, that Guy had said that we would drive along South Africa's coast looking for a cottage, dreamed that he had said he would come to New York. I was positive he'd talked about South Africa, but had he really said he'd come to New York?

I predicted that the pain would persist for a while, but neither of us would feed on it. We would both try to rise above it and get on with our lives, he faster than I.

· 53 ·

Becoming Stone. Good Stone.

The rest of my life lay waiting in New York. I went to work every day, slept in my own bed on a mattress that wasn't lumpy. I had a potato peeler, pie plates, dozens of cookbooks, fast Internet access, clothes for every occasion, and sandals in three colors, and I shopped in pharmacies and supermarkets swollen with goods. I rode the train to the city, and if I didn't want to take the train, I could take the bus. There was gas in every gas station.

Pete consoled and comforted me on my return:

Glad to hear you've made it back without brainfever or intestinal worms.

I wrote to Guy, half joking, that I would come to him wherever he was, for a while, again. If he pitched a tent in the Gobi Desert, I'd be there.

I might have encouraged him to leave Zimbabwe for New York, but did not. Beginning a new life would have been difficult for him. His presence in Harare was key to his business's success; his children were urging him to keep the house in Nyanga and hoping to remain in Zimbabwe. They didn't want to be like the many white Zimbabwean families that were dispersed across the globe. His wife was clinging, perhaps unreasonably, to the estate in Harare. I did get annoyed at his family sometimes. They were leaning hard on a man who was having regular, life-threatening hypoglycemic attacks. Didn't his wife realize the toll that maintaining the estate was taking on him? Maybe she thought he owed her; that's certainly what he thought. He told me that after all the trouble he had caused the family with his womanizing, this was the least he could do. I tried not to pass judgment on them. One thing seemed clear: his sacrifices were helping to keep the family together on their beloved estate, at least over holidays, and in their equally beloved country house.

With the failure of the Zambia contract, Guy had almost no foreign currency, and would be dependent on me for a while if he came to New York. A nine-to-five job would mangle his spirit. And what of his love of *anything female*? I would feel betrayed and furious if I sacrificed to get him on his feet in New York and then his eye wandered (as it certainly would).

He was tired. His past struggles and the diabetes had taken their toll.

Photos of Guy sat on my desk in Montclair, holding vestiges of energy, desire, and love. They gave me a feeling around my solar plexus that traveled to the right side of my neck and down my right arm. It was a craggy ache of varying intensity. That was Guy.

My mind often wandered into his frame of reference: Were there bananas in the supermarket? Were his kids okay? Was his diabetes under control? Where was he today?

But a responsible person cannot drop everything for love. I had a job, a house, friends. My son and his wife told me they were expecting my first grandchild. I could not head halfway around the world in the opposite direction at this crucial moment. I put away his photos and tried to think of other things.

The lawyer I worked with changed firms, and I hated the new one. So I quit. I wanted to spend a year figuring out what I wanted to do next—maybe teaching, maybe writing, maybe part-time work. Maybe visiting the Gobi Desert. Ernest had died in 2004, and I could take early Social Security by using my survivor benefit. It was smaller than my own benefit would be, but would help a lot—by far the nicest thing he had ever done for me, besides fathering my wonderful children. I had a small stash of savings that would see me through at least part of the year.

Robert wrote that he would be coming to New York in April. His magazine was launching over the summer and he expected to come once a month. This time he assured me he was much healthier and was really coming. We planned to meet at the statue across from The Plaza Hotel in New York. He wrote that he was searching for the proper lingerie—what color did I want? He sent me pictures of lingerie he was considering, and I chose the style that I liked the most. I did it reluctantly, because lingerie meant nothing to me and so much to him. He said it would give him great pleasure to give something so beautiful to me as a gift. At most, I was curious about what it might feel like to wear it. I had never worn such things. He said that when he went into stores he was so physically aroused at the prospect of being alone with me that he had to talk to the salesladies from behind clothes racks.

We planned to take a long walk in Central Park before getting to the lingerie. This would give me a chance to assess him up close. I was still leery about this encounter.

Two days before he was to arrive I got this e-mail from him:

Please forgive me, but I won't be there to meet you. I wish I were stronger. With love and regret,

Robert

I had affection for his ardent, vulnerable self, and was disappointed that we would not meet, but I was also relieved. He had written that since his mother's death so many years ago *my ability to love has become shallow or brittle, and when lost I just shrug and move on*, and that was the last I heard from him.

It was Robert, not a younger man, who suffered from an Oedipus complex. He was still in love with his mother, who had died thirty years before.

· 54 ·

The Wheels Come Off

Guy wrote that he missed me a great deal. *Roll on August.* The newspaper reported that instead of leveling off, Zimbabwe's fortunes seemed to be plummeting.

Guy wrote that the police were now raiding private fuel stocks, just taking them without payment. Consequently, he had fuel for only one of his company's ten trucks. Prices were going up fifty percent a month, and the bakeries had queues 500 metres long. The electricity was being cut for hours every day. It was no wonder that he was *so pissed off I cannot tell you.*

News reports said the government had displaced as many as a million of the eleven million people living in Zimbabwe. One report said that there wasn't enough fuel in Harare for planes to fly all the way to London. They had to stop en route to refuel. If I went there in August, how could I even be sure I could get back?

I kept hoping for a break somewhere—Mugabe lightening up or dying, Guy deciding to move to England or New York, the Zambia contract unexpectedly reviving.

If I had felt uneasy walking the streets of Harare when the situation was merely *almost* desperate, how wise would it be to walk the streets surrounded by people who were starving? I would be isolated behind the walls of a compound without electricity to cook or use my computer, unable even to shop for the day's provender. Guy, or Lovemore, would have to scavenge for the food. I wondered whether giving hospitality to an American, especially a writer, would put Guy in danger.

The place in Nyanga was sold to a black African hotelier a month after I left, leaving the entire family bathed in tears. We couldn't go there in August, even if we had the gas. The landlady was going to sell the house Guy was living in. He didn't know where he would be living in August, and was worried that *in extremis* he would have to live with his wife for a while, though he said neither of them would like that. Susan's abode had been leveled by government bulldozers, but Guy had found her an apartment and she was still coming every day.

Guy wrote that the market at Mbare, that teeming mass of stalls selling anything under the sun had been bulldozed. *It was like a major football pitch with nothing remaining standing.*

Several of Guy's acquaintances had been imprisoned or fined for writing e-mails unfriendly to the government. If I asked for straight answers from him, it might endanger him to write them in an e-mail. If I couldn't learn about the situation there in order to determine what I would do, what was the use in writing?

The e-mails became less frequent and more generic. On May 24th, 2005 he wrote that this was *the week that the wheels have come off.* There had been no electricity for a day and a half, and fuel, food, and basic commodities were not even available on the black market. Susan was *queuing from 3am to get to work.*

His understatement that it *presented somewhat of a challenge* was loaded with irony.

I sent him strips to measure glucose content in his blood and a glucometer, a coffee maker, two nice towels, and *The World Is Flat* by Thomas Friedman.

Greta deemed the relationship with Guy "star-crossed." This assessment struck me hard because it was dead on. My brain knew it was over, but I was not as adept as Guy at mastering my heart.

My forebodings thickened when he wrote me that he was torn between our relationship, the loyalty he had to his family, and his ever unquenchable excitement about the unknown. He said, *Handling Zimbabwe is a pure adrenaline rush.* Then the hammer came down – he had met an attractive woman, and they were finding it *quite binding to be helping each other deal with the preposterous situation.*

> *I can not see any safe and peaceful way out and so am doing what I always do look it in the eye and be honest with every one. You have been so good for me. Though I have never really been in love, I have loved people, you in particular.*
>
> *Lots of love, Guy*

I was only slightly less grief-stricken than I had been when we physically parted. She was exactly what he needed. It had broken his heart to sell his home in Nyanga, and guess what? She had a house there, near the acacia forest. If I loved him, I would have to admit that he had made the right decision.

I couldn't quite let go yet, but responded that I would not be coming back, and wrote:

> *I realized on the plane coming back from Zimbabwe what wonderful life gifts I had received there. For one, I had learned what it felt like to love someone.*

My own agenda firmed up with the collapse of my hopes (or fantasies) of seeing Guy again. Leaving one's job at sixty-three to become a writer was an entrepreneurial leap. When it comes to risk, it is second only to, say, starting a business in Zimbabwe. Guy showed me how to make an intelligent plan and stick to it. Analyze the dangers and challenges without emotion, and without turning to other people—construct it within yourself. Invest in your enterprise with an open hand. Don't be afraid. The planning takes a while, and the success comes one day at a time.

If Guy could be a successful businessman in Zimbabwe, I could be a writer in America.

· 55 ·

The Same Old Grind, Only Better

There were not just two alternatives, Guy, and not-Guy. Benjamin and I resumed our cozy, comfortable times together. He never asked more than, "How was it? Did you like it?" He didn't even say much about his own year in Kenya, right next door to Zimbabwe. It was one more thing to not talk about over breakfast. He withdrew every now and then for a week or two. Lila continued to decline. After leaving my job, I was spending all my days in Montclair, so visits to New York were all the more welcome.

I was coming to believe that "The Love of Your Life" was a myth, embroidered and expounded upon by people who had not found the loves of their lives. The best arrangement was what I had with Benjamin.

We met each others' children. He spent a couple of days over New Year's Eve with me at my brother's house in Vermont. Other than these rare exceptions, it was just Benjamin and me, pretty flowers, nice dinners, plentiful sex, easy conversation.

In December my grandson was born, and it took less than ten seconds to fall utterly in love with him. Yes, my relationship with Guy was not meant to be, and here was yet another reason why. Like Guy, my family was one of my reasons for living.

On a Friday afternoon in March 2006, I came to Benjamin's apartment in the late afternoon and we settled on his comfy couch to drink our tea, my legs sideways across his lap. "How are you?" I asked.

"I'm okay." He did not look at me. He was looking down, stroking my legs. He looked sad.

"Physically?"

"Physically I'm fine."

"Mentally, emotionally?"

"I'm not so good." He lay his head against the back of the couch, his eyes very open, nearing tears. "Ann, I don't think that I'm capable of having a relationship with you now. I don't have the energy. I just don't think I can do it right now. You are such a beautiful woman, you have a beautiful body and a beautiful mind, beautiful children, you have your singing and your writing, your lovely house, friends—you have a great life. You deserve someone who will be there for you, love you, devote himself to you. That's what you deserve. And I just can't do that. You have everything a man could want, you're so attractive, intelligent, sexual, and loving."

My first impulse was to silently pick up my bag and go home. I also had an impulse to hit him over the head with my bag.

He went on, staring at my legs as he stroked them, at my arms as he stroked them. "I miss my own beautiful body. I am carrying all of this extra weight and it's not going away. I'm not satisfied with anything in my life. I'm trying to get this book started and it isn't going the way I want it to. I don't sleep, my computer is fucked up."

As he moaned away, I stopped listening to him and began

to anticipate life without him. I would be alone again. Starting all over. Taking the year, the two years, the three years to establish a solid relationship, getting to know someone new after the initial blossoming—another cycle of pleasure, pain, and doubt. Benjamin and I had been seeing each other for almost two years. It seemed so easy now. I thought to myself, *Ann, you're looking for a unicorn, misguided by myth, hoping for a man who will 'really love you.' Even a man who sort of loves you is not working out.*

Benjamin went on talking. "Surely there will be many men who see you, your beauty and intelligence, your sensuality, and you'll find someone—no, let me put that another way. Someone will find you. Someone will find you."

"Hah." This came bitterly out of my mouth. The kitchen fan made white noise around me.

We sat on the couch in silence for a while, then I found some words. "So what do you want to do? I mean exactly. Do you just not want to see each other again?"

"I don't exactly want that. I can't have the kind of relationship with you that you deserve."

"So far this conversation is all you. I'm here too."

"Yes, I know. I want to hear what you have to say."

I was forcing myself not to flee. I was trying, Guy-like, to identify the truth of the situation. "Our relationship has brought so much stability into my life."

"Yes, and into mine too." He stroked my leg and kissed my neck over and over.

"All the social paradigms seem so empty. 'A man who will really love me?' What is that? A man who really loved me might make an ass of himself in front of my children or my friends. Or he might come to a party and mope the whole time, and I'd have to smile and be charming though I wanted to punch him in the nose. I've never known a man who 'really loved me' in the way you are talking about. I don't need this

Prince Charming character you speak of. I need stability and I need sex."

"I do too. I don't have the slightest desire to go out and find any other woman. It's not that at all."

There was no reason to avoid talking about the sensitive subjects any more, so I came clean with him about Africa and Guy. I said that I finally knew what it was like to find someone who, under other circumstances, could possibly qualify as Prince Charming. But the circumstances hadn't been right, in many ways, which still meant that finding the right match remained next to impossible. There was, in other words, always something. I told how I accepted an "open" relationship with Guy, but how that experiment had failed miserably because I had fallen in love.

Benjamin's eyebrows were going up and down quickly. "I'm so glad you are telling me this."

"I thought about telling you about Guy before I went to Africa, but you and I had not shared any commitments, so I was free to look elsewhere and didn't owe you anything. Besides, I didn't know how it would work out with Guy anyway. We might have hated each other. When I came back, the right moment just didn't come up, and then Zimbabwe fell apart, so there was no point."

"You're right. You were not required to tell me."

"I missed you while I was there, despite how I felt about Guy. I always wondered whether a steady, lighter relationship might not work out better for me in the long run. I don't want to spend the rest of my life chasing something I have no evidence exists."

He stroked me, kissed my neck.

I threw my head back over the arm of the couch, tears seeping from my eyes. "It's all just so sad. Buddha says life is suffering. I guess we just have to try to rise above it."

· 56 ·

And Now, Ladies and Gentlemen!

enjamin wanted to go out one last time, so a few days later we went to a restaurant. This was the first time that we had ever had a date outside the apartment, except for the glass of wine on the evening when we had met.

We were sitting at a high, small table in the bar waiting for them to prepare our table when an elegant man came over to Benjamin and shook his hand. "We know each other."

"Oh yes. I think I met you when I was going out with Lena. You were there with your wife."

"She wasn't my wife, but yes."

Benjamin didn't seem anxious to continue this conversation, but when the man didn't take his leave, Benjamin introduced us and invited him and his date to join us. They were on their way out, we were on our way in, so they didn't order a drink, but we all chatted for a while.

Daniel took the chair next to me, and as he sat down, he looked straight at me. He was wiry, dark, tall, intense, perhaps fastidious. The difference between other dark blue suits and his dark blue suit was the difference between a rhinestone and a diamond.

At a moment when Benjamin was talking with Daniel's date, he asked, "Are you and Benjamin exclusive?"

I was taken aback, and excited, by the clandestine advance. "Hmm. Not really."

Daniel returned to light conversation. He said he was a securities attorney who had grown up in Newark, New Jersey, in the same Weequahic section as Philip Roth. We got talking about birthdays and Daniel said his was the next week.

"What year?" I asked with a twinkle, daring him.

"1944," he riposted immediately, raising his eyebrows with a wry smile.

Benjamin joined our conversation and praised my house in Montclair. He had only been there once, but spoke of it proprietarily. *What a snob*, I thought.

Daniel nodded. "I know Montclair. What part of town do you live in?"

"I don't think I should tell you that," I teased. "You might show up on my doorstep." Benjamin joined in the laughter.

As Daniel and his date left, he said to Benjamin, "I'll give you a call," and they shook hands good night. I was impressed that several years after their double date, he should still have Benjamin's phone number. This man was a steely powerhouse.

The next morning, I packed my toothbrush, Lubriderm, little pillow, and a couple of books. Over breakfast, Benjamin was quiet, then said with tears in his eyes, "I see you have taken your toothbrush."

This time that toothbrush was going to go home and stay there.

I had a delayed reaction to our breakup. For days, I cried

myself to sleep, feeling terribly alone and sorry for myself. I awoke with tears already streaking my cheeks, found the tears pouring from my eyes as I drove to the mall, back from the mall. I had said that I would swallow the pain, but there had been so much of it, and it was pouring out of me. All the pain from all the men was welling up.

Greta was in Arizona, and I wrote to her:

> *After I left Benjamin I felt as if I were back at the beginning, right after my mother died. I started with no-one and now had no-one again. This morning I meditated. As I breathed, I felt a shaft going into my "heart." My pain was partly fear that my heart would break.*
>
> *I felt a lotus flower come from under my heart, wrapping its petals around it. You know how water plants look fragile and delicate from a distance but up close are almost like leather, thick and tough. That's how the lotus flower was. It wrapped its petals tightly around my heart to protect it. Blows would be at first deflected by the petals, then the energy of the attack would drain into the flower's roots under the water. I felt peaceful.*
>
> *Thanks for listening. I really needed it.*
>
>   *Ann*

I don't know where the lotus flower came from, but it strengthened me.

Greta called me the next day. "When I read the part of your e-mail where you said you felt you were back where you were after your mother died I laughed out loud. You're not back there. You are a different person. Be patient."

Pete comforted me: *Love? Love is like a cat; alluring, on us, imploring, often when we least expect it, then off somewhere hiding, leaving a hairball on the rug, kitty litter to be changed.*

Fired up with frustration over Benjamin, and pure sexual attraction, I thought again about Daniel. I decided to try to find him, and pored through the attorney directory, Martindale-Hubbell, looking for a Daniel who practiced in New York City and was born in 1944. It took about twenty minutes to find him. I went to the website of his law firm and wrote him an e-mail:

Subject: Our meeting late Friday

It seemed there was a lot left unsaid. This e-mail is where to reach me if you agree.

Ann

He answered:

Ann, Are you who I think you are and, if so, how did you get this e-mail address? Daniel

I answered:

Daniel, I am who you think I am. Assuming I know who you think I am.

I thought you might like to see me again, and I knew that you would never find me from the information you had, except through Benjamin, and that would go nowhere. So (having worked for years in law firms) I looked up Daniel, 1944, in practice more than twenty years, spent a few minutes investigating, actually more minutes than I had intended, but once embarked it was fun, and found you.

I know that writing you is risky because you might get semi-hysterical, but it is meant to be non-invasive. My interest is based on your clarity and agility of mind, your humor, your openness and sense of adventure, your intelligent assessment of risk, and your residence in several worlds I know well. Maybe a few other things I can't think of at the moment, like you're tall, dark and handsome.

Ann

He answered:

Ann, Very impressive. I am not the least bit hysterical, merely surprised, and yes, I would very much like to see you again. You can call me at ....

Daniel

I had never gone out with a man who wore suits like that. We made a date to meet at seven on Tuesday at Rene Pujol, a French restaurant on the West Side.

I didn't want to be a charity project, so took care with the way I dressed. I thought I looked quite chic, wearing a fitted white blouse from Nordstrom's with a beautiful peacock embroidered on the sleeve and well-fitting black pants. I even put on the pearl and diamond ring I had inherited from my great aunt Lillian.

He was waiting for me outside the door, and shook my hand. I ordered their seafood platter and had the most delicious scallop I have ever tasted, but he ate abstemiously. We talked about our children, the stock market's craziness, his pleasure at having moved into the city from New Jersey, my house, our mutual love of the theater, and my life in Greece.

He called for the check and then asked, "Would you like to see my place?"

"Sure."

We walked toward the avenue where he intended to flag a taxi, and while we were waiting he said, "I collect things."

"Really? What do you collect?"

"Antiques, mostly clocks."

"What got you interested in that?"

"I just like them."

We stopped in front of a well-lit apartment building. Flowers bloomed around the edges of the spacious lobby, and a water fountain sighed in a green courtyard.

The doorman wore a long grey coat with braiding at the shoulders, and tipped his cap, "Good evening, sir."

There was an elevator operator whose accent, when he said "Good evening," marked him as Russian, or maybe Polish or Ukrainian. I pretended that I was used to all of this as we silently rode up to the seventh floor.

My family had antiques. They had sickened of the goopy Victorian stuff, thrown it all out, and gone Early American. We'd had an antique bed warmer, old brass fireplace implements, a Colonial corner cupboard, spatterware, pewter, mirrors mottled with age, Shaker chairs, and a venerable cherry dining room table. We'd had two-hundred-year-old apothecary bottles, a collection of colonial-era tools, even two Revolutionary War-era rifles. These artifacts felt like home to me since I had grown up with them. I was intrigued to see what Daniel had, but not prepared for what I saw when we entered his apartment.

In his spacious living room, there were clocks of gold, some of inlaid wood. I learned names I had never heard, "Seth Thomas" and "Deniere." There was a ship's clock in a rich wooden case, some fobs, a gilt clock, an "industrial" clock, a couple of jewel-encrusted watches, and some tiny women's timepieces. He had begun to collect fine furniture as well, and chided me when I absent-mindedly put my water glass on an American Renaissance Herter center table featuring what I soon learned was "marquetry." No wonder he lived in such a secure building.

After a mini tour of the collection in the living room, he offered me a glass of wine, but I didn't have time to finish it before discovering that he was a voracious lover. (Before coming to bed, of course, he meticulously hung up that beautiful blue suit, put his shoes on a shoe tree, and put the rest of his clothes in a hamper.) Between bouts of lovemaking, he said, "Why don't you stay? Don't go." I could do as I pleased, so I stayed the night.

I now had another comfortable routine, only with none of the romantic expectation of the one with Benjamin. I could never live with a man who had such a collection in his living room, who noticed every hair that dropped into his sink, who arose without speaking every morning, showered, shaved, put on his thousand-dollar suit, and went to work (carefully ironed blue jeans on Saturday). Not caring deeply for him made the arrangement even better. I wasn't always wondering what he was thinking, and didn't blow a fuse when I found a silk bathrobe with embroidered roses on it in his closet.

It was months and two visits to a sex club later that I learned that he and Benjamin, and their dates, had met at a sex club.

Like the nude beach, once you took off your clothes and got settled, the whole thing was ho-hum. The easy sex made people open up, made women and men equal, and added humor and interest. What I had once learned on the Internet, I now saw in person. Easy sex made people happy.

People went to the sex club, Trapeze, for many reasons. Couples came together for variety, or sometimes to be exhibitionistic. Most of the people were middle-aged or older. They had learned that their original assessments about sex had been concocted to make people behave a certain way, like refraining from sex until marriage or smothering their interest in other people after they were married. They had learned, as I had, that biology is a ruthless commander. If not satisfied or at least appeased, life is miserable. I would not want to go back to Trapeze more than once or twice. I went for curiosity and fun, but the kinds of things I saw there were not exactly fun—they revealed the things people did in order to make life bearable.

Wow! What a replacement for Benjamin! With Daniel, I could have all the sex I could take. He told of sex clubs in various parts of the world, of paying for a transsexual prostitute, crazy women, sadistic women—it didn't much matter to him. The arrangement with Daniel was not time- or heart-consuming, and might go on for a long time.

Most nights it was just the two of us, the Mets, his antiques, a takeout meal from an excellent restaurant, and sex. He explained. "You have no idea how intense my days are. It begins when I walk in the door at seven thirty in the morning, and it doesn't end until I walk out at seven at night. By the time I leave work, I'm done." It was take it or leave it, and I took it.

One night I lifted the silk bathrobe out of the closet on its hanger.

"That's for when I feel like cross-dressing," he lied with a broad smile. He knew I knew he was lying.

Work was Daniel's mistress, not the girl in the rose kimono. He referred to himself as a "control freak," but he was not in control. Like many lawyers, he was a slave to his work.

Our relationship inched forward, growing so imperceptibly that we would both be dead before it became bigger than a breadbox.

A year into this cozy arrangement, he told me his mother had fallen very ill and we wouldn't be seeing each other for a while. That was a welcome break. I was becoming jaded.

· 57 ·

How to Get Your Wife Back

few days later, I read a posting on Craigslist by a seventy-year-old man, Jack, who wanted someone to go to the theater with. The tone of his posting was light and friendly, and I answered it. I liked the theater too.

He had posted that he was married, but his wife didn't like to go out and he would like to. There was something fishy about the posting. How could a man go out with another woman publicly without worrying about his wife finding out? His marriage was his problem, but it would also be mine if we had to keep an eye out for people he knew. It would be nice to go to the theater or out to dinner, though, so I wrote him:

> *Some company might be nice for me, too. I don't understand*
> *what sort of relationship you are proposing. I would like to*
> *go, but cannot visualize how you could be married and yet*

be seen publicly with someone else. I am not interested in a fugitive relationship.

His answer met my question head-on, which I liked:

My wife is uninterested in going out but agrees that I should not limit myself. We've agreed to a don't ask, don't tell policy.
    Any chance for coffee?
                                 Jack

I remembered Samuel, the monkey on the ground, and his supposed don't-ask-don't-tell marriage. After all the kinds of marriages I'd seen, I had to assume that some people made this work, and Jack wasn't proposing afternoon trysts in a hotel room, he only wanted to go to the theater. I would lose nothing having coffee with the guy.

The following Tuesday, I walked from my house to meet him in front of the Bellevue Theatre. A spacious blue Cadillac glided to a stop in front of me, and a trim, smiling man got out and walked vigorously around the front of his car to shake my hand. He was a couple of inches taller than I was, with thinning grey hair and a handsome but deeply lined face. He was gracious and friendly and opened the car door for me. That was a nice gesture.

"What shall we do now?" he asked, perky as a cheerleader.

"How about taking a walk in Brookdale Park?" I suggested. "It's a beautiful day."

He turned the key and the engine kicked in. "Show me the way."

Among the pink, blossoming trees in the park, conversation came easily. He was agreeably curious about my life. He claimed to run four miles every day, and he walked as if he were about to break into a run at any moment. My daily swimming laps had conditioned me as well, and our walk became a workout. He seemed a man who did nothing halfway.

The story of his life burst from him. He and his first wife had followed the rules and were both virgins on their wedding day. They had sex only once on their honeymoon, in a train on the way to Mexico, and after that, she felt her duty was done. Over the years of their marriage, he had vivid dreams in which his wife was begging him to have sex with her and he "ravished" her, half-asleep. That was how they had managed to produce two children. Good Lord!

Jack had believed that celibacy was a mark of good character, and had latched onto the myth that after marriage sex would be plentiful, so he was mighty disappointed. He entered the army a few years after their wedding and became what he referred to as a "tall dog," only not with his wife. He met women in alcohol-flooded military clubs and bars and hooked up with them in the bathroom, sometimes outdoors. He clearly expected me to find his tales of seduction interesting or titillating. I was fascinated to witness a person who had never come into the modern era where women were concerned. He said he was a farm boy from Oklahoma who'd gotten an MD from the University of Oklahoma, then gone into the army. The army sent him to Harvard for a PhD in public health, and after he mustered out, he worked in business and medicine.

He told about his children and his marriages—it turned out that the stay-at-home wife was his third. I had been divorced twice myself, and the rights and wrongs of other peoples' marriages were too complex for me to judge.

He said he had made a ton of money, though he was winding into retirement now. After three years in my lovely house in Montclair, I, on the other hand, was running out of money. I had spent almost all of my inheritance from my mother to buy the house from my brothers and was living on my savings and my first husband's $840 per month Social Security. I had left my $85,000 a year secretarial job to become a writer, and was now a published writer, but there was no steady income. The numbers were obviously not adding up—my property taxes alone were $18,000 a year. Jack could provide some small luxuries at no sacrifice to himself. His hands trembled a bit. He had filled in for his wife's frigidity by fucking everyone else. That was to be expected. What bothered me was his dismissive attitude toward the many other women—they were expendable, amusing whores, while he was just doing what guys do.

His hands trembled a bit. It turned out that he had fudged on his age in his original Craigslist posting. He was actually seventy-three, nine years older than me. All of that was beside the point. He had a breezy confidence and decisiveness about him, and a courtesy, even gallantry, which amused and pleased me. He had listened to his parents a lot better than I had on the subject of good manners, but manners were shallow markers. Perhaps he was what we used to call a "gentleman."

We drove to the Bluestone Café for lunch, and while we waited for our BLTs, he talked about his life in the army. "I'd come home from meetings, and my wife would say, 'Who did you kill today?'"

"What kinds of meetings?"

"We went into a room that was like a bank vault, with a heavy steel door that clanged shut after everyone had arrived. We didn't come out until we had done what we had to do. These would be contingency plans for operations all over the world. Most of them never happened, of course, but a few of them did. My job was to calculate how many body bags we should schedule, what kind of medics and hospitals we would need, that sort of thing."

"Wow. How did you feel about all that?"

He sat back in the booth and straightened his hands on the

table. His eyes looked past me. Slowly, tears came to his eyes.

"Why are you crying?"

"I don't know." Sobless tears were coursing down his cheeks while the waitress delivered our lunch. He turned his face away so she wouldn't see. "I just—I haven't felt this much emotion in such a long time. I can tell you things. It's—I don't know. I don't understand it."

His bathos was so unexpected and overblown that I almost laughed out loud. He barely knew me, so how could I have such a profound effect on him? Was this delayed PTSD? In reassessing his marriage, was he reassessing the rest of his life as well? Was it a crafted line of seduction appealing to the nurse in me?

I didn't bother to question Jack's stories, because how could I ever disprove them?

"Most people just—they don't do these things. It was such a responsibility for a kid. I was just a kid." He swiped his face with his napkin. "Whew. I haven't cried like this in twenty years. Probably more." He puffed out a sharp sigh as he reclaimed his composure.

After more getting-to-know-you talk, he shocked me by clanging down his coffee cup and announcing, "You're the one. I'm not looking any farther." I thought this was a dramatic way to announce that he would be taking me to the theater. He was a dramatic guy, which was fun. He was also unloading pent-up emotions. I was flattered that he had chosen me to confide in.

Instead of the theater, we went to the Metropolitan Museum of Art. He treated me to lunch in the members' dining room, which had a glorious view of Central Park. I offered to reciprocate with lunch at my house. He arrived on a beautiful summer day and we ate gazpacho and sandwiches on the back porch. Conversation came easily. My garden flaunted its blossoming azaleas, and my private swatch of forest was donning its summer coat of leaves.

He raised his lemonade glass to me, "This is our anniversary. June 4th. We'll celebrate this every year, my dear."

That was charmingly sentimental, but I barely even remembered my own birthday. Another anniversary was the last thing I needed.

He looked me in the eye, and I looked away.

"No, no, look at me. Look into my eyes for two minutes. You can time it. No looking away."

Two minutes is a long time when you are looking into someone's eyes. I ducked and bobbed my head, laughing a little, composing my face again and again into an impassive stare, all without breaking eye contact. He had made no secret that he had been a womanizer, and his seductive skills were interesting, if a bit juvenile.

Still looking into my eyes, he stood up, pulled me to my feet, and kissed me. Then we moved upstairs to my bed and made love. He placed a rubber band around his penis, which turned it bright red. I didn't know enough about how seventy-year-old men's penises work to know if this kind of circulatory assistance was required to make their penises function, but his worked fine.

He touched me the way a masseur does, without lifting his hands from my hand, my back, my neck. "I can't get enough of this," he said. "I've lived without it for so long."

It was luxurious being semi-worshipped. His profuse compliments and flourishes of courtesy were balm to a woman who was struggling to stay afloat and change her life. At the end of that afternoon, he loved me, and asked me to repeat those words back to him.

"I don't know you well enough to say that."

"Just say the words."

"This is silly."

"It won't hurt. Just say them."

"I love you."

"There. Was that so bad?"

I had corresponded with dozens of men on the Internet who were living in the same kind of marital desert, ready to explode with needy affection. After Jack let some of it out, he would tone it down, I thought.

He asked me to come with him to his home in Stowe, Vermont where the family skied in the winter and vacationed in the summer. He needed to fix something on the roof, and wanted me with him. We'd make a trip of it. We'd eat at his favorite seafood restaurants in both places. Great! This was better than going to the theater.

On the six-hour drive, we stopped for lunch at a beautiful streamside restaurant. I went to the ladies' room, and when I came back he jumped out of his seat and pulled out my chair for me. I must have shown my astonishment, because he said, "You have to get used to this kind of treatment, my dear. You should always expect it."

When we had turned onto a side road leading to his house, he asked if I would mind just ducking down a bit so I was out of sight of the neighbors. "No need to rub her nose in it," he said.

"What?" I felt a shiver of fear. Being with Jack had a frisson of Jekyll and Hyde. His bursts of adoration were pleasant, but this surprise was like the surgeon telling you as the anesthesia took hold that he was going to amputate.

"It wouldn't be helpful to us if my wife found out that I brought you here. You know what I said: 'Don't ask; don't tell.'"

"And you know what I said! I don't want a fugitive relationship." It was funny how clearly we remembered our first exchange of e-mails. "That was *our* contract, and now you want to renegotiate it when I have no options."

"Uh oh. I can see we've got a problem," he said, and pulled the car over. He turned to me, putting his arm around my shoulder. "I'm sorry. You're right. Maybe I was a little impulsive—I wanted so much to show you the house because I love the place. Can you do this just this once? If it's too difficult, we won't come again."

I felt like getting out of the car and walking home, but I couldn't do that, so I just looked at him.

"Really, I apologize. My wife will make our life hell if she learns I brought you here. Because of the neighbors, you know, it would be humiliating to her."

My eyes closed, my lips pursed.

"Look," he gently lifted my chin. "Look at me." I opened my eyes and he gave me one of those piercing looks. "I love you. Some things you just know right away, and I knew right away that I loved you. You are who I have been waiting for all my life. Just do this for me this once, and it will never happen again. I just don't want anybody to get hurt."

I heaved a great sigh. "This is not okay."

"I know. I know. All right." He turned back to the steering wheel and put the car in gear. "I guess my idea won't fly. Let's find a hotel."

"No. That's silly. I'll do it, but don't ever ask me to do this again."

We spent most of our two days there out of the house, and he treated me to wonderful meals and pastoral walks, accompanied by flourishes of adoration and respect.

On the drive back to New Jersey, he asked if he could spend two days a week with me. "I obviously can't spend the night, but we could have most of the day together."

"We could try that," I agreed. I didn't want anybody moving in on my territory, but two days probably wouldn't impinge too much.

The following Tuesday morning, he arrived at my house at eight, while I was still in my nightgown. "I just couldn't wait to see you," he explained.

After breakfast and a long walk, we saw *The Devil Wears*

Prada. Jack held my hand, put his hand on my knee, or moved his shoulder over to touch mine, never losing contact.

"What did you think the movie was about?" he asked as we walked down the stairs.

"Doing the right thing," I said.

When we emerged into the sunlight, Jack wiped away tears with the back of his hand.

I was touched. There appeared to be something about being with me that allowed him to open up and go deep into his dark crevasses. Maybe he really did love me. "Why are you crying?" I asked. I hadn't seen anything in the movie that was worth crying over.

"I'm crying about doing the right thing. About how hard it is to do the right thing."

As we walked up the hill, he started talking aloud to himself about how he'd have to start making more money, and phoned somebody in Washington DC about a consulting job. I was baffled.

Back home we lay down for a nap. He seemed restless and disoriented and started talking again. "My wife gets mad at me for not putting napkins on the table when setting it for dinner, not vacuuming the inside of the car when I wash it, leaving a ring on the counter top when I decant the wine, not making the bed. One morning I told her, 'Should I make a list of all the things I do *right?* I do most things right, most of the time.' Sometimes, really, I think I should make a list of all the things I do right. Then she couldn't shout at me."

I sat up and looked down at him. "Jack, you're a doctor, and you're going around making lists of the times you correctly put napkins on the table? Give me a break."

"I usually remember. I almost always remember." He didn't seem to be listening to me.

I got scared again. He wasn't making any sense.

I was trying to figure out how to help him when his cell

phone rang. He reached for it on the bedside table and looked at the display. "It's my wife. I guess I'd better take it."

Without looking at me, he took the phone and went into my closet. The closet door was only about five feet from me, and I could hear her shouting, though I couldn't make out the words. I resented the intrusion of verbal violence into my closet. From my first marriage, I knew how after a while shouting becomes the regular order of things, almost unnoticeable. I sympathized with Jack, but couldn't deal with my melting from the love of his life to a little pool on the floor. Like the Wicked Witch of the West. Poof! She's gone.

He listened for a long time, then said calmly, "We'll talk about it when I get home." She kept shouting, and he interrupted her sternly—"I said we'll talk about it when I get home"—and clicked his phone to end the conversation.

I said nothing as he came back to bed. He was in no shape to answer any of my questions.

"She wants to know who I took to the members' restaurant at the museum," he said. "She knows what restaurants I go to. She knows it must have been something special."

"How does she know you went there?"

"She looked at the credit card bills. She saw the charges from the trip to Vermont. Everything. You know I was careful about splitting those charges, putting them on separate credit cards, but she figured the whole thing out. I'm screwed."

Anger flared in me as I realized how inept he had been at covering his tracks. He had manipulated me masterfully.

"I've got to go home and see if I can straighten this whole mess out. I'm not looking forward to it, but I don't have a choice."

"I thought you had an understanding with her."

"I thought so too, but I guess I was wrong."

"This is a pretty big thing to be wrong about."

He stood back and put his hands on my shoulders. "I don't

know what's going to happen, but I want you to remember this. Do you hear me?"

"You're standing right here, of course I hear you."

"I love you. Remember that. I love you."

The next morning he woke me at eight with a phone call. "Hi. It's Jack."

"How are you?" I was still coming awake.

"Miserable."

"What's going on?"

"She's been screaming and yelling all night and all morning. I can't tell you what it has been like. She's out at her lawyer's now. I'm going to have to go through all of this again." I assumed "this" was another divorce. "I don't know if I can take it. I don't know if I can take striking out a third time. I don't know what to do. I can't see you any more."

"What?" I wanted to kick him when he was down. I spat out, "So much for 'I love you.'"

"Yes, well . . ." He let his breath out with a painful sigh. "When she comes back she's going to make me call you and break up with you in front of her. And I've got to do it. So I just want to let you know so you can answer the phone or let it go into voicemail."

He was a pitiful, drowned rat. I was furious. "Your marriage was the first thing I asked you about, and you misled me. You said you and she had an understanding."

"She says I misunderstood her. She's just fanatic, crazy now."

I began to speak, but stopped.

"I'll call you when my bridges are burned."

"Oh no. I'm not waiting around for you. Not a single day."

"No, huh."

"Bye."

"Good-bye, Ann. I'm sorry."

Boom. He was gone, with a body blow that left me reeling. Searching for the last word, I wrote him:

I feel like you callously threw me over a cliff with no concern whatever for my welfare. You dumped me without a word of solace or grace. Only a feeble, "I'm sorry, Ann."

He answered:

Ann,
What evolved was just so far from what was available. You are vulnerable on account of your honest and needy nature. The flip side of every strength is the mirror weakness.

J

What a patronizing sonofabitch. He seemed to have disdain for me for having fallen for his line.

There has been a cascade of public figures caught cheating on their wives. The list is long: Jesse Jackson, Henry Hyde, Strom Thurmond, John Edwards, adulterous evangelists, entitled politicians, far too many to ever conclude that any of the cases was an anomaly. The man apologizes to children, wife, colleagues, supporters, and friends for the horrible thing he's done, but mentions no concern for the woman he loved, the woman he said he would take care of, even the woman whom he told not to have an abortion when she got pregnant with his child. I had thought my disdain for the pontificating nabobs of "family values" could not intensify, but in Jack I had uncovered a moral abyss that sucked me in.

A few months later, he wrote me that he still felt horrible about having misunderstood the "don't ask, don't tell" thing, but that he and his wife had worked it out. She understood that *sex once a year left me nothing to be faithful to,* and that *while her physical condition continues to deteriorate, it doesn't interfere with her sexuality.*

He had used me to get his wife back in his bed.

I missed Guy more than ever—his clarity and honesty were

proving hard to replicate. Seeing Jack grovel before his wife disgusted me. I wanted a free man like Guy, whose manhood was where it belonged, not in any woman's pocket.

DANIEL CALLED ME the day after Jack's last "I love you." The affair with Jack had started and ended between Daniel's phone calls. It was very handy to have him show up again. Daniel and I had a clear contract that worked.

· 58 ·

A Last Good-Bye

Jack's callous dismissal sobered me up. I had been born, bred, and brainwashed to expect romantic love—a concept that historians say is a new one in history. It is difficult—for me, anyway—to view romance as a utilitarian tool used to accomplish procreative or business goals: the Princess of Here marries the King of There, and they establish the Kingdom of Here-There. What did people do without this brainwashing, I wondered? Or did they ever do without it? The great tales of love—Bathsheba, Cleopatra, and poor, willow-drowned Ophelia—involve tragedy and loss. The Taj Mahal was built out of grief at the loss of love. Surely these were true loves. Maybe love in times past was only for the wealthy, a luxury like sugar. From the tragic way those loves turned out, I'm not sure they would be worth it. Only fairy tales show lovers living happily ever after.

It must have been just as painful for ordinary people to leave the people they loved as it was for me to leave Guy, yet for reasons of survival, young people had to marry not the person they loved but the person who could bring a few cattle or a piece of property into the family. A friend from India told me that arranged marriages often turned out very well, so maybe true love sprouted from shared interest and intimacy. I sometimes wished someone had gone to the trouble of arranging for a suitable husband for me. They would have done a better job than I did.

After finding many kinds of love, from wispy to full-blown, and losing them all, I found that lotus flower that thickly protected my heart. I began to feel the connection to the waters around me and to let life, pain, love, everything flow through me, like water, like air.

Even when I was in a stable relationship, even in the early, content stages of my two-decade-long marriages, the pit of my stomach gripped me sometimes. The grip was a hope for salvation—the hope that a magic force would sweep into my life and, like the Wizard of Oz, place a screen between me and my problems while the wizard fixed them. Or perhaps it was fear of loss—that some day I would be a bag lady, friendless, cold in winter, eating what other people found it in their hearts to give me. The lonelier, poorer, and more desperate I became, the less they would feed me, for humans shy away from illness and despair.

I felt like the mice in my Montclair backyard who ventured out every day to find sustenance, knowing there were predators abroad. There was no way we could get what we needed without venturing into human nature, where there were inevitably hawks, sharks, and spiders. We must learn to expect them, and accept the capriciousness that sometimes had it that we would be eaten alive.

• • •

IT WAS THE SUMMER of 2006. I still felt close to Guy, and called him every six months or so. We spoke as dear friends. He said the glucometer I sent him had changed his life for the better. His attacks were far fewer, and his health greatly improved.

When I called him in June, a year and a half after I had left Zimbabwe, he spoke slowly, haltingly, and could not find some words. He couldn't remember his son's major at the university. "Oh Guy, Guy, how can you forget this," he said, frustrated. "Just wait a minute and let me think." I was alarmed. Every hypoglycemic attack had cost him a massive number of brain cells, and after so many years, some parts of his brain seemed to be deteriorating. "Well, I can't think of it just now."

"How is your health?" I asked him straight out.

He hesitated before answering. "It is what it is. There's nothing to be done about it." I was upset, but there was no one to tell, and nothing to do about it. He was no longer my problem. I would not spend my treasure to keep him supplied. He had children in New York, Cape Town, and London. He would have to ask them, though I imagined his pride forbade that.

We didn't love each other enough to leave our families, our homelands, our careers, to be together. Maybe if we had been in our twenties we would have, but leaving my children and grandchild, at the age of sixty-three, to join a lover in crumbling Zimbabwe was a different equation. There was nevertheless a nuance and depth to our love that stunned me sometimes, as if looking at a work of art.

Whenever I rocked my towheaded grandson, smelling him, touching his satin skin, feeling his dependent, soft spirit bond with my bones, I knew that I had done the right thing. Guy and I had in common our devotion to our families, and that was the very thing that kept us apart.

I had told Guy I would join him wherever he was, even if he set up a tent in the Gobi Desert, and I would have—but I wouldn't have sold my house to go there, and I would have come back home after a while.

In our June phone call, we talked about his upcoming trip to England in September for his son's wedding. I wondered what it would feel like for him to drive into a gas station and fill up at will, to see the shelves of the supermarket stuffed with goods that you could pay for without a wheelbarrow full of bills, to move about freely, to flick the light switch and know it would work. I hoped it would be a reminder that life didn't have to be the way it was in Zimbabwe. Maybe he would finally get out of there. Guy wasn't ruminating about such things, though he was amused at my ruminating. He would take it all, he said, as he took everything—one day at a time.

When I asked about his relationship with the woman he had written me about, whose name, I learned, was Rosalyn, he said that his landlady had sold the property on Drew Road, and he had moved in with her. "It seemed like the logical thing to do. Where would I have gone? We're helping each other get through this thing."

It slapped against my cheery tone to hear this, but I didn't let it show. "Good. I'm happy that you've landed on your feet."

"Yes, well." He hesitated for a moment, and my heart caught. Did he miss me? Was there still hope? If I was annoyed at myself for having a fantasy with Dr. Jack, how much greater was the fantasy with Guy? "We are muddling through. It's just, you know, the thing to do right now."

Pangs and aches accompanied every conversation with Guy. His hesitation when talking about Rosalyn might have had a meaning between the lines, but I was afraid enough of the pain of hope that I didn't pursue this, even to myself. I didn't offer to meet him in England.

As I knew from my time in Zimbabwe, Guy's schedule was very regular. He asked me always to call at 6 p.m. his time, after the office staff had left, and in late September, when I calculated he would be back from his son's wedding, I called him, but there was no answer. A week later I called him again. I was burning with curiosity to know how it had felt to eat a juicy steak with good wine, to have fresh milk and vegetables, and to have real money in his pocket. It was odd that he wasn't in the office at 6:00 twice.

I called a third time, this time during office hours, and the young woman on the phone stumbled when I asked for Guy. "Oh Medem, oh, I suppose you are not aware that he has passed on."

"Oh no!" I cried out. "Oh no. Oh no."

"I'm so sorry, Medem." The secretary was flustered.

"What happened?" I was terribly roiled and distraught, but did not want to make the secretary uncomfortable, so I tried to speak calmly.

"He wasn't feeling well one afternoon and left the office early."

"He never used to do that."

"No. It was quite unusual. And later that night he had a massive heart attack."

He was gone, at sixty.

I asked to speak to Guy's personal secretary of twenty-five years; she had been visiting her daughter in Brazil when I visited Zimbabwe, but I knew that Guy had told her about me.

She gave me more details. The rascal died in bed, thank God, and was found by the maid the next morning. I wondered if it had been Susan, but supposed that Rosalyn had her own maid. Rosalyn was away, so he died alone.

He only attended church for social reasons, and God did not figure in his worldview at all, so I asked him once about how he would want his body dealt with when he died. "You think I care? That will be up to my sons to decide." He was cremated.

When I put the phone down, I lifted my hand, palm up, and could almost see ash in it. Dust to dust. Ashes to ashes. Our choice. Guy's beautiful body is ash. My mind saw his toe suddenly begin to disappear into ember, like a newspaper fed to a growing fire.

I didn't know what to do with myself. My friends knew about Guy, but they didn't know Guy. We had no common acquaintances. There was no place to mourn.

Sadly (tragically, I sometimes think), Guy and I had to part, caught in history's pincers. Neither of us had years to wait for the world to turn right-side up again, so we constructed our lives without each other, but there was always that little thought that we might see each other again somewhere, at least for me.

Greta had recently become a Celebrant; her business was creating rituals for all sorts of occasions, but mainly weddings. She had studied Native American culture and had lived in many countries, so had a wide-ranging view of the purpose and form of ceremony. When she answered my e-mail telling of my grief over Guy's death, she suggested that I devise a ritual to mark his passing. I dedicated a well-loved Brahms Intermezzo to him, and played it dozens of times, like a prayer. It is haunting, contemplative, slightly dissonant. Brahms instructs the pianist to play tenderly, pianissimo, and I try each time to play it more tenderly, more pianissimo.

· 59 ·

Keeping the Good Stuff

wondered if I could incorporate what I most admired in Guy into my own self. Could I look at my situation as coldly and intelligently as Guy had done during our morning conversations? He had a remarkable ability to remove himself from the field and make an assessment without involving his heart. Coldly, intelligently, where was I now?

A year after leaving my job, I was getting threadbare financially. I would have to start making money. When I got my MA in English in 1964, I had intentions of teaching English at the college level, and maybe getting a doctorate, but wanted to travel before beginning my career. My "travel" lasted thirteen years, and after I returned to the US I had two children to raise, then after divorcing Ernest I had to scramble to feed and house myself and my kids. So I became a well-rewarded legal secretary for twenty years. What a perfect circle it felt like when I began teaching writing at Montclair State University in 2006, forty-two years after first deciding to become a college professor! The freshmen in my classes were spirited, intelligent, and utterly unprepared for college. I became attached to them and loved my work.

With so many other good things happening, my search for a companion diminished. In the absence of love, sex was available. My attention turned to my friends and family, my garden, my writing, and my job. Singing and playing the piano took back their places in my life.

I answered e-mails and contacted new people on dating sites from time to time, but couldn't gin up any enthusiasm for the men I was meeting. I kept in touch with Ken, Benjamin, Frank, and Howard. Guy, alas, was dead, and Jack was back behind the walls of his marriage. Pete and I wrote as intimately and supportively as ever, maybe once a week, maybe less. *I have come to think you are my mirror image*, he wrote. We still hadn't met.

I wanted to move to Manhattan, where everything vibrated a notch higher. I saw the lights of the city out my front window, and they beckoned, as they always had. I would try to sell my house and move to the city. I would meet new people. There was the gulf of the Hudson River between me and the numerous single men on the Upper West Side. From the attitudes of Benjamin and other correspondents, I realized that living in Montclair had made me geographically undesirable for many men.

Around this time, I began to read poetry. I found images and forms in poems that I found nowhere else. Once graduated from the *roses are red, violets are blue* level, poems fed me truth and beauty. All the old rules, all the old social castes and categories, all the old expectations were vapid. Those old rules served people who wanted to be protected, shielded from reality, and comforted. Only the truth would comfort me now.

There was no "normal" anymore, there was just what was. One poem haunted me for days, "The World Loved By Moonlight" by Jane Hirshfield. She wrote that we had to *become colder* because *only something heartless could bear the full weight.*

I had been taught to be soft and caring, but what was needed was hardness, tolerance of pain, of weight, of grief. Only when I became hardened could I support the truth and beauty I was seeking.

One morning in the fall of 2006, I took down a large file folder from my bookshelf. It was a foot thick, the elastic straining to hold it together, the accordion sides stretched so wide that they were tearing at the outer folds. Inside were printouts of hundreds of e-mails from or to me, grouped in paper-clipped bunches, one for each correspondent. The first one was dated August 2003. Some bunches were so large they needed a heavy clip or a thick rubber band; others were a single page.

Though the oldest letter was only three years old, I had forgotten some of the men who had written these e-mails. The woman who had written and received them was also a stranger. Did she have no limits? Where were her morals? Why was she talking with total strangers about fetishes? Where did she find the time to write hundreds of pages of e-mails? She was so hungry for undifferentiated experience!

The relationships in these folders seemed so unusual, so unlikely, so against the accepted grain. Despite my many adventures, I was still not sure that women in their sixties were supposed to have such adventures.

I wondered if I could re-create the story these pages told. Was my experience just a fluke? I published a Craigslist posting as an experiment and clicked on the "Send" button at four in the afternoon.

In or near the Upper West Side (63)

In 1950, when I was 8, I did some calculations—I would be 58 when the year 2000 rolled around. It seemed to me then that I would be near death. Instead, it's 2006 and I'm wearing the same size clothes I wore when I was 21, swim 30 laps almost every day, feel a sense of freedom and excitement that fears I had when I was 8 kept me from feeling. It would be delicious to find someone to enjoy this wonderful life with. Age is unimportant (as far as I am concerned). Steadiness and spontaneity go together very nicely for me. Solvency would help so I don't have to pay for everything, and a zest for whatever it is we did together, including, sometimes, doing nothing.

My mind is open.

The first response arrived at 4:15:

It's not that I have the older woman thing persay but as a very fit and attr man in his 40's I find an exciting mature woman can be very sexy. Bill

And another at 4:20:

Good afternoon, my name is Bob, I am 43, 6'2, and 235 lbs. I am very intrigued. .

One sent me a poem:

Give me your deepest morning hug
Your moon face that drabbed the blue skies
Give me back the golden days of pure love

And another:

*im a younger guy who enjoy intimacy with a older
woman.*
*if you need to be
loved let me know*

And another:

*I was 53 when Y2K turned. pic below is Nov '04 on a boat
delivery south.*

Within twenty-four hours there were forty responses.
One man was twenty-nine, three were in their sixties, and the
rest were evenly spaced in their thirties, forties, and fifties.

Yes, these adventures could happen again. They had cost
much in time, anguish, and money, but they had forced me to
change, and that was what I'd wanted. None of the responses
piqued my interest, but I felt relieved that the choice was mine.

Daniel and I were seeing each other again, under exactly
the same circumstances. He wasn't melancholic or suffering
from guilt or shame, like Benjamin, so I had the feeling that
our trysts could continue indefinitely—but I had thought that
before. That rose kimono stayed in his closet.

He had the perfect attributes for an attorney: reserved
enough to enjoy achieving success through his clients'
successes, perfect discretion, intelligence, perspicacity, and
ambition. I assumed that he could relax with me because he
had come to realize I was not coyly looking for a way to get
him to spend his impressive earnings on me, or to marry me.
He let down his guard a bit, confided in me about his work and
his family, and became more playful.

One night he gently, but a bit sharply, slapped the side of
my face with his open hand.

I instantly grabbed his hand and tried to slap his face in
retaliation. "Hey! What do you think you're doing!?"

"You're going to be my bitch," he pretend-threatened, and we wrestled over the bed as I tried unsuccessfully to slap him back, both ending up convulsed in laughter.

"What did you do that for?" I wanted to double-check that he wasn't serious.

"I don't know. Just felt like it. Do I take it that you don't, after all, want to be my bitch?"

I couldn't help but laugh. "You can make Miss Rose Kimono your bitch."

He made a mock grimace. "Oooooooh. Low blow."

I was in no position to castigate him for seeing another woman. We turned it into a joke.

From the way he appeared to enjoy telling me about his previous adventures (though not the rose kimono), I got the sense that he sometimes felt lonely, though he never said anything even approaching that. He had the most bizarre stories, like the woman from Colorado whom he had met on the Internet. She'd flown to New York to spend a weekend with him, and she'd asked him to tie her up, bite her, and hit her hard—*hard*.

"I guess she came all this way so she could be far away from people who knew her," Daniel surmised. "She probably has some respectable job somewhere and she doesn't want other people to know she loves getting beaten up. I just couldn't do what she wanted."

"And what happened in the end?"

"I told her I couldn't see her anymore and she wrote me a really nasty letter."

"Hmmm."

"A real nut case. I don't need any of those."

I enjoyed coming into the city a couple of times a week. He didn't want to talk in the morning, so I left his apartment at seven, was home by eight thirty, and carried on with my own life.

We didn't love each other, but we were becoming pals, and he was becoming a habit with me. My cynicism about ever finding true love, whatever that was, was deep-seated. I considered myself lucky to have found someone I could enjoy, with a minimum of demands on my time and interests. I could see Daniel and still feel like a free woman.

I corresponded with men who responded to my profile, but before Christmas 2006, eighteen months after my first date with Daniel, I started feeling I was wasting my time even looking at Match.com, Yahoo!, American Singles, and Craigslist. Most of the profiles were familiar by now. I grew to recognize the writing styles of men on Craigslist, I realized that the new postings were mostly just the same men posting with a different story or request. In Daniel, I had what I wanted.

· 60 ·

The Unicorn

On the off chance that there really was such a thing as true love, and that I was missing out on something, I decided to join just one more website, one that didn't feel as go-go as the others. It was connected with *New York Magazine*, and I envisioned readers of the magazine—Upper West Side professionals, I thought—subscribing to it.

One photograph showed a gray-haired man named Terry with a striped scarf around his neck and a pleasant and inviting expression. He was looking slightly downward. The profile said he was six feet tall, a professor who loved reading. His favorite books were *A Hundred Years of Solitude*, *The Mars Trilogy*, and *Reading Lolita in Tehran*. He had never been married, had no children. He was a Mets fan. I absorbed the good feelings emanating from this person for a few minutes and wrote him a little e-mail:

Just because we are both professors doesn't mean that we have anything in common, but it might be interesting to find out.

He responded. Since it was almost Christmas and I'd be away in Vermont, we agreed to meet after New Year's. He remembered which day I would get back and called me. He was paying attention to me.

In early January, 2007, I drove into the city to meet him at a restaurant on 9th Avenue, just past the Lincoln Tunnel. There was more than one construction site in the neighborhood, and thus no parking places, so I had to pay for a parking garage. As I walked toward the restaurant I was in a bad mood —why had I decided to continue on this time-consuming and expensive quest? What would it take to get it through my thick head that the lure of true love was a mirage, or even more than a mirage, a lie?

To get to the restaurant from the parking garage I had to walk by the apartment of a just-retired Cornell sociology professor I had gone out with a month or so before. On our second date we'd walked miles and miles down the Hudson River on a lovely Sunday afternoon, had a nice dinner (we split the bill), and read each other poetry in his Upper West Side apartment. He'd called me after I got home that evening to tell me, "Really, Ann, don't depend on me. I'm notoriously unreliable. I wouldn't want you to think that I was really, you know, available. I've already been married twice, and really don't think I could get married again."

I had known the man two weeks and been out with him twice! "I wasn't aware that I was expecting to marry you."

"You know what I mean. I don't want to mislead you. I just want you to know."

He then apologized for being so "stupid," and said he was going away to Panama to bicycle through the jungle with his son for six weeks. At the end of the phone conversation, he told me he had just been diagnosed with prostate cancer. I was shocked, and before I had gathered myself to express my sympathies, he abruptly said good-bye.

Why was I going back into the lion's den again? When would I learn!?

I was a little early, so I stood in front of the restaurant and tried to calm down. I had made a date with this pleasant-looking man, and wasn't going to turn around and go home, so there was no reason to allow irritation left over from a previous date—and from parking woes that were not Terry's fault—to ruin what could conceivably be a nice afternoon.

I watched the dozens of people crossing the street and coming down the block: a clown with a big nose and floppy shoes on his (her?) way to work, a scoliotic old lady with a tiny dog, two giggling Hispanic girls whose ample bosoms protruded from their raincoats, an awed family from maybe Minnesota? Ohio? Out of the corner of my eye I glimpsed a man walking catty-corner across the avenue toward the restaurant. He was overweight, but carried it well. He had an unhurried gait, and the same pleasant, friendly look as his photograph. It was certainly him. I felt calmer just looking at him.

We shook hands and began an easy conversation. I looked *up* at him. Up! How nice. The first restaurant was full, so we went to Rosa Mexicana, across the street from Lincoln Center. The place is always packed, but on this evening we were taken straight to a table—a good omen, I thought. The wall to the right of the stairway had water flowing down it, spraying just a bit on the people walking up the stairs. There were tiny figures of divers at intervals on the water wall.

Terry ordered a pomegranate margarita, and I ordered a Negra Modelo beer. A smiling waiter rolled a table into place beside our table and prepared fresh, piquant guacamole, crushing together the avocado, salt, tomatoes, and cilantro in a bowl made of black volcanic rock.

As we talked, I had my eagle eye out for deal-breakers, but after three hours of conversation had uncovered no Other Woman, Lingering Regret, Financial Catastrophe, Unrealistic Expectations, Romantic Attachment to His Mother, Signs of Mental Illness, Religious Fanaticism, or Republican Leanings. I considered it a good sign that he had had a couple of serious relationships. He had no children, was solvent, employed, socially skillful, affectionate. He was a couple of years younger than I was, and in good health. Where was the blow from left field?

I could not believe my good luck in meeting somebody who was potentially normal, so I Googled him when I got home. The first thing that popped up was his university home page, with the same photo as had appeared on the dating website. He had been Teacher of the Year in 2004! That was a stamp of approval from a lot of people.

Quite a few delicious dinners later, some made by me, some by him, some by his chef friends in their restaurants, some in new restaurants, my birthday came up and he took me back to Rosa Mexicana. By then he was spending several nights a week at my house. Still no deal-breakers.

We had been anticipating their great guacamole and sat back to enjoy a margarita and a Negra Modelo as we waited for it. We sat next to each other rather than across from each other so we could touch knees under the table and hold hands between courses.

"I got a new bra," I told him. "Just for you."

"Really?" He seemed tickled. "Tell me about it."

"I'll do better than that. I'll show you." I folded down my blouse to reveal the lacy top of the bra.

"Umm." He bent forward with a big smile and folded the blouse down a touch more.

When we sat back, the young waiter had arrived at our table and was mixing the guacamole with a huge smile on his face. He assiduously attended to the guacamole, but we all knew he had seen our flirtation. I put my hand up to my face in embarrassment, and Terry sat back in his chair with a smile. The waiter said nothing as he placed the guacamole on the table, but couldn't wipe away his smile.

After dessert, Terry said he had a special birthday present for me.

"This dinner is pretty special in itself. Thank you."

"No. Something more."

"Okay. What is it?"

"Tell me anywhere in the world and I'll take you there for two weeks."

I took the proposition as a joke. Most men I had dated wouldn't so much as follow through on "Let's have dinner soon." My doubt must have showed. Was this going to be the Bullshit Deal-Breaker?

"No. Really. Where would you like to go? Where is it that you've always wanted to go but never thought you'd be able to?"

"Hmm. I haven't really let myself think in that way. Australia?"

"If that's where you want to go, that's where we'll go."

"That's really far to go for just two weeks. No no. I should choose a place where I have never been. Thailand? Tahiti? Maybe Hawaii."

"Hawaii would be nice. I've been there once. I had my pilot's license at the time and flew all over the islands."

"We could stop and see my daughter in Los Angeles on the way." I kicked myself for suggesting that. I didn't want to appear unable to enjoy things without bringing my children into the picture, but it did seem so sensible. We'd have to stop somewhere between Newark and Hawaii.

"Okay. Whatever you want."

Enter the Deal-Breaker

Although he had never been married, Terry wasn't a loner. He had a close-knit group of six friends who had been sharing dinners, holidays, and vacations together for decades. They had drunk good wine in France, Ireland, Florida, and New York, and had shared each other's flaws and successes. They were politically liberal, generous, a bit eccentric, and tolerant. They welcomed me into the group without hesitation, and I enjoyed their company. I considered it a privilege to drink Corton Charlemagne, Grange Hermitage, Chateau d'Yquem—some of the best wines in the world—and to eat at some of the world's best restaurants in their company. My life as a *bon vivant* began.

I wondered why he was still a bachelor at sixty-three. One by one, his past relationships surfaced: One woman had died of cancer while they were engaged, and that had taken a long time to get over. Another engagement had faded after he moved to California for two years.

He, like Benjamin, was regularly interrupted by phone calls on his cell phone from someone with whom he had spent many years. He explained that he and Helen had been living together for twelve of the last fourteen years, more like family than lovers. They had finally separated two years before, though Helen was having a difficult time and called him regularly. He wanted to do what he could to help her.

She was a brilliant artist and writer, had gone to both Harvard and MIT, and was highly eccentric and a difficult person to live with, he said. He was delighted by her differentness, her explosive talent, and her unapologetic self-expression, but ultimately tired of her constant demands, her misery, her aggressive attacks on him. When his friends referred to her there was sometimes a slight rolling of the eyes.

I could barely sit still as he told me about her. I was weighing every added bit of information against our ease with each other, our common profession and view of the world. At what point would this dream sink like a stone? It was sounding more and more as if this was a situation I wanted nothing to do with.

It wasn't the difficulty of being around Helen that had ended their relationship, though, he went on—it was her "gender dysphoria."

I had a vague idea what he was talking about; some kind of discomfort with one's gender. Did this mean Helen was gay? I had two friends whose husbands had turned out to be gay, and that was a particularly bitter pill. Was she a transvestite? Did it mean she was trippy and bouncy like RuPaul, or confidently mid-gender like k.d. lang, or miserable and nasty? I was forcing myself to keep my mind open, though my instincts were screaming at me to flee.

"What, exactly, is that? I mean, I can imagine, but tell me more."

"She always felt that she should have been a man. Even as a child. It caused her all kinds of mental and emotional problems, and, eventually, physical problems as well."

I got the impression that this was his take-it-or-leave-it statement. I would have to live with the presence of Helen if I was to make a life of any sort with Terry. That had also been the deal that Benjamin offered regarding Lila.

We were sitting at my kitchen table. I leaned on my elbows and put my head in my hands. Terry sat still and watched me without any apparent emotion.

After a minute or so, I sat back in my chair. "I don't know where to begin with this one."

Terry said nothing, just watched me closely.

"I mean, it's not as if *you* were transgendered. So what does it mean?"

"You can ask me any questions you want about it." He was feeding me information fully, without excuses or elaboration.

"Okay. When did she decide she would become a man, and what's her, or his, name?"

"Bruno."

"Bruno? That's so macho."

Terry laughed. "I don't know why he chose it."

"When did this gender change happen?"

"It developed gradually, starting a couple of years into our relationship, though, really, it had been developing all of her life."

"And then what did you do? I mean, you still lived together?"

"We weren't having sex by then, but she continued to live there. There were a couple of breaks when she, then he, lived elsewhere, but until two years ago, he had his own room in my apartment."

"You didn't have any clue about her dysphoria before that?"

"That's hard to say. We had our problems. But it really started bothering her about three years in."

"And where is she, or he, now?"

"He's moving back to New York. He's been in Princeton for a while."

"And how often do you see each other?"

"Almost never. But we stay in touch by phone."

It was as if Benjamin's relationship with Lila had been a training run for this. I tried to be analytical and Guy-like about it. The important flaw in my relationship with Benjamin was not his phone calls with Lila, but his own melancholy and defeatism. Terry showed none of that. He was steady as a rock, had never shown himself overcome with regret or crippling memories, and had never withdrawn from me for a single day. Phone calls from Bruno did not send him into a funk. Wasn't that the most important thing?

"I've had so many crazy people in my life. It's daunting to think of adding one more."

"You don't have to add Bruno."

"I don't think I want to."

"That's okay. He is struggling, and I feel a responsibility to help him. He calls and talks and talks. It's not as if I am suffering myself. I just feel responsible to a certain point. As if he were a prodigal son, maybe."

"Do you give him any money?"

"No."

"I don't know what to say right now. This is a bit of a surprise, you might say."

"Think about it." He paused for a few moments, looking at me intently. "I want more than anything to make this relationship work. If you have any more questions, ask me. I won't let it interfere with us, but I won't stop talking with Bruno either."

"I understand."

There was the Deal-Breaker.

I thought about it for the next couple of days. I was hardly perfect myself. I was healthy, working, and still engaged in the world, but a man could certainly find a younger woman if he wanted. I had left a good job to write, and so far had nothing to show for it but a steadily declining bank account and a few pieces published in the literary press. I had children and a grandchild who would in many situations command my first loyalties. I had been married and divorced twice, which, in my case, meant that I was capable of making disastrous decisions at times. I was skittish about marriage and commitment, and was going out with other men, with no signs of giving them up. I thought that my perpetual motion would also be a deal-breaker for some people.

Terry had many wonderful qualities, one of which was loyalty. He was loyal to his long-time friends and to Bruno, and would probably be similarly loyal to me if I became ill or disabled, or did something inexcusable. Bruno's sufferings were partially of his own making, and partially the result of a mental illness that might have been totally unrelated to his gender issues. I could not be sure how I would have handled it if I had been dealt the cards Bruno had been dealt. Maybe a bit of compassion was in order.

On the other hand, I would be very unhappy if my life was once again strongly influenced by the chaos of another's mental illness. Mental illness is infectious in a way, and I didn't want to be exposed. People who live around mentally ill people find themselves doing bizarre things to accommodate.

But there was Terry every day, being as good to me as a man could be, as thoughtful, as attentive, as generous, and as loving as I could ever want. He was holding nothing back. I sat on the fence as I became more and more attached to him. Bruno called from time to time, sometimes at very inconvenient hours—eleven at night, eight in the morning—and talked on and on, but Terry kept those conversations out of my way. Chaos did not enter my life, but I was watchful.

· 62 ·

The Proposal

Three months later, after our semesters were over, Terry and I left for Hawaii. It was the first time since childhood that I had not been responsible for the travel arrangements. Even when I was married, I still handled the trips. When my teenage children and I were in France, years before, the rental car went dead somewhere between Nice and St. Tropez, and in Paris I nearly ran out of both money and balance on my credit card and had to figure out how to feed two ravenous teenagers without scaring them about temporary bankruptcy. Every other trip had been stressful in other, unique ways.

On this trip, I was no longer perilously in charge but felt lower to the ground, safer. Someone else was worrying, and I was grateful. I sympathized with Terry's edginess as we checked in—patting his pocket to be sure he had the boarding passes, getting the slightest bit snappy with the clerk when he said that our airplane seats had been changed.

The visit with my daughter went very well, and then we flew to Honolulu.

Our huge bed at the B&B near Waikiki had previously belonged to Princess Ruth, a four-hundred-pound titan of the Hawaiian aristocracy. I lost Terry in it a couple of times. In the room was a desk almost exactly like my grandfather's antique desk that I had sold a year before. Terry said the oriental carpet in the bathroom was the precise pattern of his oriental carpet. It was eerie.

On our first morning in Honolulu, the birds frantically greeted the day outside our window. Birds were everywhere, either invisible in thick vegetation, placidly visible like the small soft grey doves that sat as if on an egg in the middle of the road, or wild high flyers claiming the huge skies near the sea. The trees were unfamiliar. What was that enormous spreading tree with the gnarled, aboveground roots and the dry-looking tentacles hanging from its branches. The tree with sideways-reaching branches as long as my house is tall was a double-pod acacia, I learned. It didn't resemble the African acacia in the forest near Nyanga.

Nature itself seemed upholstered. The spacious, open, covered porch, called a lanai, was ten feet from our room, barely visible through the foliage. There were similar wide verandas in Zimbabwe, where the weather is also temperate. The four-foot-deep couch on the lanai was as comfortable as a chaise lounge. Was it outdoors or indoors?

Adapting to changes in privacy etiquette is one of the more interesting aspects of traveling. In Europe, I sometimes felt violated by people's standing "too close" to me, their faces and fingers "too close" to my face or chest. In Zimbabwe, I had to figure in servants, who were always nearby. In Hawaii, the windows were wide and open. There were even open, screened windows in the bathroom. Privacy was secured by visual blocks, such as huge plant leaves and draping vegetation.

Normally privileged sounds, like those coming from the bathroom, were dispersed there, as sound streamed ceaselessly from all directions. As Terry and Sumiko, the housekeeper, chatted outside the bathroom, my peeing was just one of many sounds they heard, though I felt exposed.

We ate the breakfast of half a papaya, mango, pineapple, strawberries, bananas, a hard-boiled egg, toast with exotic marmalade, and asparagus wrapped in cheese and ham. Sumiko's precise and tidy hand was everywhere. The owner of the B&B, a middle-aged woman with roots in Illinois, was a pack rat whose overwhelmed but tasteful hand was also in evidence.

On our last night in Honolulu, we visited on the veranda with Sumiko. The house was so blended with its vegetation that the exact shape of the house was difficult to discern. It had taken me two days to realize that Sumiko lived in a small room off the kitchen. She had lived there for decades.

"How long you been married?" she asked.

"We aren't married," I laughed. "In fact, we just met."

She slid her eyes over to Terry. "Why you don't make an honest woman of her?"

He smiled. "Do people always have to get married?"

"It's better that way," she said.

"Did it ever occur to you that maybe *I'm* not the one who objects to getting married?"

I was surprised to hear Terry say that; Sumiko burst out in merry laughter, and the subject was dropped.

On the island of Kauai, we stayed in a modern B&B, built on twenty-foot stilts to avoid devastation when the next hurricane blew through. There were three guest rooms, each named after a different fruit. Our room, the Pineapple Room, featured the color yellow and a round bed.

The hostess, Kirby, taught me how to tie my pareo, and I wore it around the B&B. On a neighborhood walk, I passed an old Hawaiian woman wearing a pareo sitting in the front yard of her house, almost camouflaged in the heavy foliage around her. She wore a lei around her neck, and smiled warmly, white teeth in dark skin. The pareo looked just right on her, but I would have felt fake wearing it outside the B&B. Terry liked it for sure. Maybe he was jealous and wanted to wear it too—it was so comfortable, and so easy to get in and out of.

On our last night there, we visited with the host, Toby, over a beer at the bar. Toby had arrived from Wyoming twenty-nine years before with a bicycle, $450, and the intention to proceed to China, but never left Hawaii. He didn't like his given name, Milton, and so named himself after his dog. Toby elaborated on his theory that the World Trade Center was an inside job: Bush and Silverstein. He had a pocketful of stories—how he and his wife, Kirby, were both arrested by the same policeman for speeding on the same stretch of the coastal highway one night, how they stayed home and got drunk instead of evacuating when the last hurricane passed through.

Terry had taught me how to play the ancient Asian game GO, and we brought along a portable GO board. Toby watched us play. He had never seen anyone play GO, but suggested some sharp moves against my GO Master, Terry. "Thanks," I said. "I'm just beginning, and can use all the help I can get."

"She beats me sometimes. She's smart," Terry remarked.

"Yeah?" Toby winked at me. "Why do you think he married you?"

"He didn't," I said. "We're not married."

"Oh!" Toby laughed. "Okay!"

"Your move," I reminded Terry, who was looking out the window.

"What are the rules?" Toby puzzled as he turned his attention back to the GO board.

"The rules are"—Terry paused over the board—"if she loses three times straight, then she has to marry me."

The subject was dropped again. Marriage? The mere word had, until now, created a shiver of antagonism and terror along my spinal cord. This time it created a little ember of excitement. Terry was warm and substantial, physically and in every other way. I felt a constant presence at the other end of the seesaw—I would not flip off it with him there.

On our last day in Hawaii we were tired of living in everybody else's world, so we just took a nap and lazed around. We watched the end of the Yankees-Mets game and the Preakness. It felt good to do something we would ordinarily do at home. After dinner we lazed some more in the hot tub, which sat outside in the yard beside the B&B. The evening was warm and the stars were richly present. There was nobody about so we took off our bathing suits and let the soft air and warm water pamper us. I missed my normal routines, and was ready to go back home, but in Terry I had part of my home with me, and he said he felt the same way about me: comfortable.

That summer, we visited friends in Vienna, staying most of the time in their ultramodern house outside of the city. We swam in their pool, made them dinner one night, went to a concert in the Musikverein, played with their kids, and nearly broke our necks in their bathroom, which was all glass and tile —beautiful, but very slippery.

Design was a challenge on this trip. So many things were beautiful, but how did they work? The blinds? The light switch? The lock? The faucets? Each one took a little study to master. Form did not always follow function. Terry loved form; I loved function. The shower in our Prague hotel had a glass partition across only half of the opening to the rest of the bathroom, causing water to flood the floor during an enthusiastic shower. One answer to this problem would be less enthusiastic showers, but that was not a solution in my view. I did not like the architect to dictate to me how I should take my showers. The hotel solved the problem by heating both the floor and the towel racks. The towels were necessary to wipe the water off the floor so we didn't slip, so drying them quickly on a heated towel rack was a good idea.

These mental challenges both reduced and heightened my abilities to play GO. I lost abysmally and won handsomely, though usually I lost, which was as it should be, since Terry had been playing for thirty years and I was just learning. We played on the dining room table of our hosts, in the train, in hotel lobbies. It was a wonderful diversion. If I was overwhelmed with impressions and reactions, my mind was not within my control, and it showed in my GO game. Playing GO was as good as any medical test to show if my brain was working well.

We continued eating at intriguing restaurants, trying out those with a good reputation. In Prague, we ate at Klub Architektů, an arched stone cellar below a building where there are architecture exhibitions. The food was adorable—I had lamb steaks with prunes, raisins, and rose chutney with slices of orange, tomato, and cucumber on the plate. I ordered "typical Czech potato dumplings," which were pure white slices of moist potato bread that soaked up the gravy voraciously. The separate side dishes were a challenge. All salads and vegetables had cheese or a rich sauce of some kind. My solution was to eat only half of my portion, and to only taste the broccoli, cauliflower, and carrots with Dutch Cheese Sauce. Terry's lamb steaks (they call them "steaky" in Czech) had a bilberry sauce with "wild spices." We tried each other's dishes, and they tasted pretty much alike: meat smothered in heavy, sweet sauce. Of course we had to try dessert too, but by that time we were clobbered with sugar and could only manage a bite.

Back in Vienna, we wandered through the streets, stopping at Mozart's house, where I got my favorite baseball cap, with "MOZART" on the brim, and bought an extravagant goose down pillow on which I still gratefully lay my head every night.

Over lunch in a sunny café, we agreed that Terry would live in my house full time. He didn't want to give up his apartment in Hoboken, but we'd figure that out later. We began to discuss what-ifs.

"We'll work this out," he reassured me. "We might get married, if you want to. I might even like it myself." He said no more but smiled and watched for my reaction, a glass of fine Austrian white wine in his hand.

I was silent for a while as a flash of decisions banged around in my head. I didn't like having Bruno around, but Terry had not let him interfere in our own relationship. I remembered a friend who had lost everything when her boyfriend of eighteen years suddenly died—his family had come and taken the house, the car, the bank accounts, everything. I wouldn't want to run a risk like that. Terry and I never argued (a tiff now and then, but nothing lingered), my children liked him, my friends liked him. The answer poured out of my mouth unbidden. "We could have a hell of a party."

Terry laughed. "Then we'll do it. It's up to you. If you want to, we will."

"If we are going to stay together, I definitely would want to get married. I don't want to live in 'life partner' land, the no-man's land where nothing is anything. There are too many people involved—my children, your friends. Besides, we're not exactly twenty-five." We talked about changing our wills.

A few weeks before, we had visited my son, and when he was introducing Terry to a friend he'd hesitated: "This is Terry, my mother's"—pause—"Gentleman Caller." What, indeed, does one call one's mother's boyfriend? "Boyfriend" was too juvenile. "Partner" would require an explanation, "life partner" sounds sterile, "lover" makes people laugh. "Husband" held in it all the things I would want to tell the world about us. Walking along the street in Vienna arm in arm, Terry complained, "I'm being demoted from Gentleman Caller to Husband."

"Yes. You're becoming the conventional husband. I don't get any particular thrill from doing things unconventionally, like living together and not being married. I mean I wouldn't do that only because I wanted to be different, not that it's so different these days."

"I like being unconventional," he said.

"Then we can have an unconventional marriage," I suggested, and we both laughed.

We had bought our airline tickets separately and would take different routes home, so Terry and I got on the train in the Vienna railway station, he in one car, I in another. Cars would be detached in the middle of the night, with his going to Milan and mine going to Rome.

In the middle of the night the train stopped, and I felt gentle bumps and heard muffled voices as they disengaged the part of the train carrying Terry. There was a brief blackout as they rebooted the electrical system. I felt as if an arm had been wrenched off as they separated him from me.

ROLLING THROUGH THE ITALIAN countryside the next morning, I could feel my life settling into a very comfortable spot. I reflected that never before in history would I have been able to do what I had done over the past few years.

I would certainly not have been hired as a university professor at the age of sixty-three.

A hundred years ago I might have been chained to Ernest forever—or, if I had left him, I would have been branded a divorcee and probably would not have found another husband, especially not in my late forties.

Until political changes made social services available, what would I have done with Tom, a mentally ill husband? I would then have been chained to him, even if it was worse for him as well as for me.

Until relatively recently in history, at least in the western world, I would not have been able to own property, work outside of the home, have my own business.

Without the technology of the Internet, I would never have met Ken, Frank, Howard, Bruce, Guy, Jack, or Benjamin. There are tales, like *Der Rosenkavalier*, of older women having love affairs with younger men, but the affairs are treated as gossamer fancies. After the dozens of e-mails I received from younger men, I have to conclude that some young men have always been attracted to the stability and substance of older women, but socially, it would have been out of the question. I might have met any of these men at a party or at work, but without access to the intimacy of the Internet, we would not have connected. Without the Internet, I would not have met Guy, or come to know him so well. Not so long ago, Zimbabwe would have been as inaccessible as Mars to the ordinary American, and as a woman, I would not have been able to travel there alone.

Not so long ago, sixty was old. I would probably have covered myself in modest clothing, contented to crochet for my grandchildren, as my great aunt did, or belong to the Garden Club and church groups like my grandmother.

The only thing that wouldn't have changed going back to the beginning of humanity was my yearning to see my darling again.

· 63 ·

True Love

Greta married us on the first day of December, 2007, slightly less than a year after we met. Terry is generally allergic to churches, so we chose the restaurant owned by friends of Terry's. We agreed on a playlist for the dining and dancing, and a friend brought her viola to bless us with some Bach.

Greta and Fred flew in from Arizona the night before the wedding, so Greta did not have much opportunity to look over the final changes in the words we had written for our ceremony.

Family and friends came from Virginia, Upstate New York, Rhode Island, Brooklyn, Vermont, Connecticut, and various parts of New Jersey, fifty-five guests in all. At the appointed time, my dear family and friends were seated before the antique dresser with flowers on it that served as an altar. The children were restless, and some of the adults had driven a long way and seemed tired.

Greta suggested that we include our "love story" in the ceremony. I thought that was a good idea since many of the people in attendance did not know exactly how the wedding had come about.

She began to read from the text. "Before Ann and Terry met, they had each been dating wildly . . ." She hesitated, we all hesitated, then the room exploded in laughter. She had misread "widely." Greta was mortified, then she melted into laughter too, blushing and apologizing profusely to me and Terry, all of which was drowned out by the loud laughter, which went on for what seemed a very long while, led by the bride and groom. The restless children settled in, the tired long-distance drivers relaxed, and the edge went off the day. It turned out to be, as I had predicted, "a hell of a party."

THESE DAYS, Ken and I speak on the phone two or three times a year. He tells me about his children. I continued seeing Daniel for a while after we were married. He lived near the church I was going to then and we had dinner after choir practice, but our habit was to have sex, and without it, there wasn't much to talk about. After a month or so I e-mailed him to say I wouldn't be seeing him any more, and he answered, "You will be missed."

Michael has had health problems; we speak from time to time, but his promises to visit don't come about. Pete had been a mentor, supporter, and advisor, and now that I had pretty much figured it all out, there wasn't much to say. Around our correspondence there had always floated an unfulfilled flirtation, and that was gone now. By sheer coincidence, I once met Guy's sons at a concert, but what was there to say? I told them I missed talking with their father, but they didn't know of our close connection, and I certainly wasn't going to tell them how much we had loved each other. It was painful to meet them as strangers when I knew so much about them. Frank and Howard said they were sorry we would be losing touch. I wished them all well.

Without comment, Terry has let me arrange my friendships

with old flames as I wish, but it seems wise, loving, and right to let them go. I miss the delicious liberty of celibacy, but have added far more contentment to my life than I have taken away.

I WOULD HAVE TO give up too much fabulous food and wine to weigh 145 pounds again. My extra eight pounds is not too much of a sacrifice for such delights. Terry loves my tummy. He has a tummy too, and the way he is made has become the way things should be.

Two months after our wedding, our granddaughter was born. As we drove to meet her for the first time, Terry said, "For an only child who's never had any children of his own, this will be a new experience."

I breathed in the smell of the newborn child, thrilled to her silken skin, and then placed the swaddled baby in Terry's arms. Her head wobbled alarmingly and abruptly, and he scrambled to secure her. I flashed back to my first moments holding my newborn son. I feared I'd break the baby, but my pediatrician reassured me, "Babies are made of rubber and steel." Terry held her at a distance from his body, as if using his engineering training to calculate the best angles for maximum support, then carried her into the kitchen, where the light was more muted. I watched this tall, robust man shift his arms to hold her tiny body more securely and watch her every twitch and stretch for the longest time.

I felt like Odysseus. After my risky outbound journey, I knew about the siren songs, abysses, bewitching spells, and strange monsters that were out there, but they sank out of sight in the fulfillment of my homecoming. Terry might only be her step-grandfather, but this baby would feel us both as her grandparents. This love was forever. Even after we were gone, it would still be around.

I was contented and, well, in love.

Acknowledgments

Every writer needs discerning readers brazen enough to say what is right and wrong with one's manuscript. Not readers who say, "Move the comma," or "Gee, I really like it," but experienced readers who get at the heart of the matter. I have been privileged to know several such people. My husband, Terry Stoeckert, and my friend and fellow author, Carolyn Niethammer, have read from the beginning. Lisa Romeo provided solid coaching halfway through this project. I have been meeting once a month for five years with fellow writers Phoebe Hoss, Marilyn Mehr, Betty Walker, Carol Emmerling, and Carolyn Jackson, and I am grateful for their astute, frank, and skilled assessment of my work. My attorney, Fred Ferguson, gave me more help than he was paid for, and Joelle Delbourgo and Debra Kass Orenstein provided important information when I needed it. My appreciation of course goes out to the men who shared these experiences with me. And under it all, I don't do anything without being grateful for my inspiring children.

In this new, baffling world, SheWrites Press has figured out a publishing model that works. I thank them for that.

Your Dating Workbook

Maybe you are dating or thinking of dating, or perhaps
your mother or your daughter is. Here are some ways of
thinking about this. Think bluntly, indulgently.
Nobody is watching.

- **Definition.** An Austrian friend once asked me, "What
  is dating? I don't think we do that here." Every culture and
  every person has a unique definition. What is yours?

  ....

  ....

  ....

- **Etiquette**, including sexual etiquette.

  How do you find people to date?

  Who makes the first move?

  If asked, where would you suggest going on a first date? At
  what point would you invite him/her to your home?

  What form of sex takes place at what point in the
  relationship?

  ....

  ....

  ....

- **Goal**. Why do you want to date? Take some time to elaborate. Your dates might fit in any of the following categories.

  Fun Partner. A one-time or occasional meeting to watch a sporting event or maybe you got some free tickets to the opera. It's not exactly dating, but relationships can sometimes develop.

  Companion. A more regular presence, such as someone who shares your pleasure eating at fabulous restaurants, a bridge partner, or a regular hiking buddy.

  Friend with Benefits (sex without commitment). What are your requirements and what are your terms? What is your availability? Include safe sex guidelines.

  Committed relationship or marriage? What are your criteria for a partner? Non-negotiable requirements? Areas you don't care about?

  ....

  ....

  ....

- **History**. Review your dating or marital history. What were your greatest weaknesses/strengths as a date or partner? Do you want more of the same kind of person you have been involved with before, or something different? Did your choices of partner also bring you closer to your friends and family? Whose advice has been helpful?

....

....

....

- **Keep a Journal**. Write down your developing thoughts and experiences, and go back and review what you have written every few months.

- **Keep a Budget**. How much time and money are you spending on dating?

....

....

- **Pros and Cons**: This may take off some of the romantic edge, but can help keep your feet on the ground. Consider what qualities might be listed when evaluating yourself. Maybe you want to compare one person with another, or create a list of your own priorities. Here is my list:

Requirements	Deal Breakers
Sane	Addicted
Solvent	Mentally ill
Kind	Practical joker

About the Author

Ann Anderson Evans is a writer, linguist, and professor. Her writing has been published widely in both literary and academic magazines. Featured on the Discovery Channel's *Sex in America* in 2012, she was also on the cover of *Eldr* magazine's issue on "Sex and Intimacy over the Age of Sixty."

A wife (for the third time), mother, and grandmother, she has traveled widely and lived in Spain, Israel, Italy, Austria, Germany, and Greece. She speaks six languages.

Her website and blog are at www.annandersonevans.com. She is on Facebook (Fan and personal pages), LinkedIn (Ann Anderson Evans), and Twitter (@annwriter).

An audio book of *Daring to Date Again* is available through her website and elsewhere.

Contact: Jennifer Prost Public Relations
973-746-8723 phone | 973-746-8759 fax
jprostpr@comcast.net

SELECTED TITLES FROM SHE WRITES PRESS

Flip-Flops After Fifty: And Other Thoughts on Aging I Remembered to Write Down by Cindy Eastman. $16.95, 978-1-938314-68-1. A collection of frank and funny essays about turning fifty—and all the emotional ups and downs that come with it.

Her Name Is Kaur: Sikh American Women Write About Love, Courage, and Faith edited by Meeta Kaur. $17.95, 978-1-938314-70-4. An eye-opening, multifaceted collection of essays by Sikh American women exploring the concept of love in the context of the modern landscape and influences that shape their lives.

Seeing Red: A Woman's Quest for Truth, Power, and the Sacred by Lone Morch. $16.95, 978-1-938314-12-4. One woman's journey over inner and outer mountains—a quest that takes her to the holy Mt. Kailas in Tibet, through a seven-year marriage, and into the arms of the fierce goddess Kali, where she discovers her powerful, feminine self.

Peanut Butter and Naan: Stories of an American Mom in the Far East by Jennifer Magnuson. $16.95, 978-1-63152-911-5. The hilarious tale of what happened when Jennifer Magnuson moved her family of seven from Nashville to India in an effort to shake things up—and got more than she bargained for.

Americashire: A Field Guide to a Marriage by Jennifer Richardson. $15.95, 978-1-938314-30-8. A couple's decision about whether or not to have a child plays out against the backdrop of their new home in the English countryside.

Loveyoubye: Holding Fast, Letting Go, And Then There's the Dog by Rossandra White. $16.95, 978-1-938314-50-6. A soul-searching memoir detailing the painful, but ultimately liberating, disintegration of a twenty-five-year marriage.

CPSIA information can be obtained at www.ICGtesting.com
Printed in the USA
BVOW05s1635300914

368852BV00003B/9/P